What W. H. Auden Can Do for You

Writers on Writers

Philip Lopate
  Notes on Sontag
C. K. Williams
  On Whitman
Michael Dirda
  On Conan Doyle
Alexander McCall Smith
  What W. H. Auden Can Do for You

What **W. H. Auden** Can Do for You

Alexander
McCall Smith

Princeton University Press
Princeton and Oxford

press.princeton.edu

Jacket illustration and design © Iain McIntosh.

ISBN 978-0-691- 14473-3

Library of Congress Control Number: 2013938077

British Library Cataloging-in-Publication Data is available

This book has been composed in Calvert MT Std and Minion Pro

Printed on acid-free paper. ∞

Printed in the United States of America

10 9 8 7 6 5 4 3 2 1

Contents

Author's Note

This book may be about a personal reaction to the work of W. H. Auden, but it nonetheless owes a great deal to the efforts of those scholars who have, over the years, created a significant body of critical literature dealing with Auden's poetry and other writing. I have benefited greatly from the insights of those critics. Anyone writing about Auden, though, must owe a particular debt of gratitude to Professor Edward Mendelson, Auden's literary executor and the author of two magnificent accounts of his work, *Early Auden* and *Later Auden*. Professor Mendelson generously read the manuscript of this book and noted several points that needed correction; responsibility for any remaining errors is, of course, entirely mine. I also enjoyed many conversations with Professor Mendelson over the years, including a number of such conversations in Scotland during the much-appreciated visits that he and his wife, Cheryl, made to us. I am most grateful to him for the light he sheds on even the most obscure of Auden's lines; no poet, I think, could ever wish for a better guardian and exponent of his work than Professor Mendelson. I am also grateful to Professor Alan Jacobs for writing his wonderful book, *What Became of Wystan?* That book helped me greatly in understanding a number of aspects of the poet's development.

What W. H. Auden Can Do for You

1

Love Illuminates Again . . .

In the early months of 1940, with Europe embarking on what was to prove the greatest conflict of the twentieth century, W. H. Auden, a celebrated—and controversial—English poet who had recently moved to the United States wrote a gravely beautiful poem. It took him some time, as this was no brief ode dashed off in a moment of inspiration—this was over one thousand lines, carefully and studiously constructed. Its title was "New Year Letter," and it was addressed to Elizabeth Mayer, a refugee from the depredations of Nazi Germany, a translator, and a close friend. Like many of his works, this poem is conversational in tone but contains within it a complex skein of ideas about humanity and history, about art, civilization, and violence. At the end of the letter, though, there occur lines that are among the most beautiful he wrote. Addressing his friend, he draws attention to what she brings to the world through her therapeutic calling:

> We fall down in the dance, we make
> The old ridiculous mistake,
> But always there are such as you
> Forgiving, helping what we do.
> O every day in sleep and labour
> Our life and death are with our neighbour,
> And love illuminates again
> The city and the lion's den,
> The world's great rage, the travel of young men.

These lines are about the person to whom the poem is addressed but when we read them today could be about Auden himself. He would never compliment himself, of course, but I believe that he is clearly one who is forgiving, who helps what we do, and if there is anything to be learned from his own work, it is precisely this message: that every day in sleep and labor, our life and death are indeed with our neighbor. And yes, in reading his poetry we see love illuminating our world.

It is this view of Auden's work that has prompted me to write an entirely personal book about the poet, about the influence he has had on my life, and about what this poet can mean for somebody who comes fresh to his work. I believe that if you read this poet, and think about what he has to say to you, then in a subtle but significant way you will be changed. This happened to me, and it can happen to you.

This small book does not purport to be a work of criticism. It does not claim to shed new light on a body of work that has already been extensively examined. It is simply an attempt to share an enthusiasm with others who may not have yet discovered, or may not have given much thought to the work of, Wystan Hugh Auden, generally known as W. H. Auden, the man whom many consider to be one of the greatest poets of the twentieth century. It is not a hagiography—it recognizes that Auden has been taken to task for trying to be too clever, for using words for effect and without real regard to their meaning, and for being juvenile. There are other charges against him: in particular, he was famously criticized by the poet Philip Larkin for turning his back on political and social engagement in favor of the self-indulgent and the frivolous—a criticism that has lingered and is still occasionally encountered.

Some of these charges—particularly the ones that accuse him of using language for effect—have some basis, but those of frivolity are certainly not justified. It is true that he deliberately turned his back on the leadership role to which English intellectuals had elected him in the years before the Second World War—the Auden age, as some called it—but he by no means sought refuge in private reflection. His later poetry, although not overtly political, was very much concerned with the question of how we are to live and by no means evades profound issues. Of course some of the poems are better than others, and we can all agree that there are some that should never have seen the light of day, but what poet or novelist has not done at least something that is best forgotten? "We fall down in the dance . . . ." Some writers have written whole books over which they, and sometimes their readers, would prefer to draw a veil. None of us is perfect, and Auden was a self-critical man who was in many cases his own severest judge, describing some of his poems as meretricious and worthless. Interestingly enough, even poems he rejected have, in the minds of his readers, survived this disowning. He wrote a poem called "Spain" that he considered dishonest, and yet it is still read—and appreciated—in spite of its exclusion from the official canon. Similarly, "September 1, 1939," has survived its author's judgment that it was a poem that he was ashamed to have written. This raises complex questions about aesthetics and the genuine. If a work of art gives pleasure in spite of the insincerity—at the time—of its maker, then does that detract from its value?

That question arises only in relation to a small number of Auden's poems, but it illuminates a larger point about Auden's work. Auden was a poet who changed. It may seem trite to say that his life was a journey—whose life isn't?—but in his case we can see his poetry respond to the salient challenges of his times. This is enlightening, not the least for anybody who feels—as many of us perhaps do—that we are living in a time of heightened flux and crisis. How should we respond to the challenges that this provokes? Most of us want to lead a good life—however that is defined. Auden wanted that too, and the solution he found might help us today. But what was it?

2

Who Was He?

Many of us can point, I believe, to a particular artist—whether he or she be an author, a painter, or a musician—and say: *This person's work means a very great deal to me.* Sometimes, indeed, we might go further and say: *This person has changed my life.* Alain de Botton has written a book called *How Proust Can Change Your Life*, a title that I suspect was devised with at least some tongue in cheek but that speaks, nonetheless, to a very real possibility of personal transformation. The title of this book is in a way lighthearted homage to de Botton's remarkable book. But something that is lighthearted can be very serious in its intention. I believe that reading the work of W. H. Auden may make a difference to one's life. Of course we can be changed by reading or listening to something that moves us deeply, that makes us see ourselves or the world in a different light. It may be a poem that has this effect, or it may be the contemplation of a great painting; it may even be the great Proustain novel itself. In any event the work of art we are confronted with unlocks within us the recognition of something that had escaped us before. We are changed because we now understand something that we did not understand before.

For me, the person who has had this effect is Auden. Who was he? One of his poems begins: "A shilling life will give you all the facts." Well, here are the facts, in even less detail than one might expect from a shilling life. Auden was the son of an English doctor. The family tradition was that the name was of Icelandic origin, although this has been the subject of dispute. When you look at a photograph of the poet as a young boy, though, he looks the part—large-boned, with a shock of light-colored hair, and that almost translucent skin that one sees in many Scandinavians. He was born into a comfortable home in which scientific inquisitiveness was always present. He grew to like rocks and old machinery, and the words that went with such things. The atmosphere in the home was one of tolerance—

at least on his father's side. His mother was less accepting of her son's ways, complaining of his untidiness and, in one splendid attack on his "intemperate ways," his habit of eating any food he came across. She herself was described by some who knew her as an unattractive and domineering personality in contrast to the milder and more accepting nature of Dr. Auden. There may be no book on the mothers of poets, or artists in general, but it might one day be written and would be, I think, an enlightening read.

As was common in those days—and still is, to an extent, in his particular class of English society—he was sent off to boarding school. Gresham's School is in a small town called Holt, in Norfolk, a remote part of rural England. Unlike many boarding schools of the day, the regime in this school was reasonably liberal and did not involve the cruelties in which the English educational system of the time excelled. These could be profoundly distorting: how many lives were ruined by a harsh regime of relentless conformity, enforced by physical punishment; how many young men were sent out into the world emotionally crippled by a system designed to produce a stiff upper lip and an acceptance of hierarchy. The English were unwittingly cruel to their children, which is something the Italians, to think of one example, have never been. Auden did not have to contend with the traditional boarding school ethos—Gresham's was no Eton—even if he felt that the Gresham's honor-culture had the curious effect of creating what he considered an atmosphere of distrust. It was a good atmosphere, perhaps, for the production of spies, and indeed Auden was a near contemporary at Gresham's of Donald Maclean, one of the so-called Cambridge spies (along with Blunt, Burgess, and Philby). Another contemporary was the composer Benjamin Britten, with whom Auden was later to collaborate. Both of those names—Maclean and Britten—can be seen today on the boards in the hall at Gresham's that list those who won prizes. Auden's name was added much later, recording the fact of his appointment as professor of poetry at Oxford.

It was while he was at school that he began to write. He had gone for a walk in the countryside with a boy called Robert Medley, an independent spirit for whom Auden felt undeclared love. They had become involved in a discussion about religion when Medley suddenly said to Auden: "Tell me, do you write poetry?" We can picture the scene: two boys walking in a Norfolk field, when one asks the other whether he writes poetry, and the other suddenly realizes that this is what he wants to do. This may reasonably be seen as one of the great, crucial moments in the arts, akin, perhaps, to the moment when it was suggested to Shakespeare—as it might well have been—that he might care to write a play about a prince of Denmark; or when Picasso's attention was drawn to the bombing of a small Spanish village called Guernica; or when Leonardo da Vinci asked his model to smile—enigmatically, if you wish, but please smile. Fortunately, Auden acted upon the suggestion, and shortly afterward he had a poem accepted for *Public School Verse*, his first publication and the beginning of an output that was to produce numerous volumes over the years.

He went on to university, to Oxford, to Christ Church, where he was the clever undergraduate, the center of a circle of like-minded bright young men impatient with their elders—as bright young men have to be—and eager to become part of the new intellectual climate that was emerging in post–First World War Europe. It was a time of intellectual and artistic ferment, and in the eyes of his contemporaries at Oxford, Auden was very much in the vanguard of all this. He was also extremely promiscuous, picking up other young men with undisguised enthusiasm, even succeeding, as one of his biographers reports, in making conquests on the short train journey between Oxford and London. But if the world seemed bright and full of possibilities, there was a snake in the garden, and this would soon make its presence known in an unambiguous fashion.

Auden was not involved in politics at Oxford—his interest in the subject was really kindled only after he left the university and went to Berlin. But many of his contemporaries were becoming deeply involved in political debate: the future they envisaged was one in which justice and freedom would be secured by the enlightened reform of society on rational principles, while material needs would be catered for by scientific progress. It was a fairly conventional left-wing vision, and it had all the confidence that such views of the world usually have. For some, such as the British intellectuals who famously traveled to Moscow, the Soviet Union became the embodiment of their hopes ("We have seen the future—and it works," enthused the fashionable social theorists Sidney and Beatrice Webb of their carefully stage-managed visit to Russia); for others the battle was a more domestic one, to be fought through unions and internal reform. For all of them, though, the greatest threat was fascism, which was threatening the very basis of European civilization. It was against this backdrop of political threat that Auden spent the years immediately following his graduation from Oxford.

In 1928 he went to Berlin, where he stayed until the spring of the following year. This was a very important experience for him in terms of political education and personal discovery—the equivalent, perhaps, of a dramatic gap year today. Christopher Isherwood, his close friend, recorded that period very strikingly in his *Goodbye to Berlin*, a book that was so successfully and atmospherically translated to stage and film. Later he went to Spain, another focal point of the battle between European left and right, intending to drive an ambulance in the Spanish Civil War. (Auden was not a good driver at all, and the fact that he did not actually drive an ambulance was probably a good thing for those whom he might have conveyed.) One of his great poems, subsequently disowned, was "Spain," in which he explores—meretriciously, he later said—the significance of Spain to his generation. There was a visit to China with Isherwood to record the implications of the Japanese invasion, and a journey to Iceland with the Northern Irish poet Louis MacNeice. Several volumes of poetry were published—to considerable critical acclaim. As a poet, Auden was feted. His was a new and exciting voice that seemed to capture the hopes—and anxieties—of the time.

In January 1939 Auden and Isherwood went to the United States, leaving behind an England on the brink of war. Their departure at such a critical time was the subject of adverse comment, with some regarding it as an act of retreat, of personal cowardice. In Auden's case, it was probably not cowardice: those who knew him are firm in their rejection of that charge. When war broke out, Auden did contact the British Embassy and offered to return, to be told that only skilled people were needed. Yet for some reason that remains unclear, he did not respond to the subsequent urgings of friends who encouraged him to help with the British war effort. In his defense, it must be said that he did not go to America specifically to escape Hitler, nor did he preach appeasement. His decision to emigrate was based on a combination of factors, including the desire to be part of a society that was still in the process of creating itself. He also wanted to earn his living by writing—something that he felt would be more achievable in the United States. And that proved to be the case: Auden always worked hard for his living and was proud of the fact that he made poetry pay.

His reputation in the United States grew steadily. He lectured widely and wrote numerous essays and criticisms. In the decades following the war, his position as one of the foremost poets writing in the English language became assured.

He returned to Christianity, to an idiosyncratic form of Anglo-Catholicism, having been influenced by his extensive theological reading and by his own need to find a way forward in life. He wrote libretti for operas, notably *The Rake's Progress*, over which he and his long-term partner, Chester Kallman, collaborated with Igor Stravinsky. He spent summers in Italy and then in Austria, where he bought a house an hour from Vienna. In the United States his home was in St. Mark's Place, in Greenwich Village, and he lived there, in conditions of famous mess, until he decided to return to Oxford, where he was given a cottage on the grounds of his old college. His last years there were spent in an Oxford that had changed significantly since his own undergraduate days. He was a lonely figure, sometimes sitting alone in a coffee house, untalked to by students who were too shy to do so or who were simply unaware of who this shambling, unkempt figure was. He was seen in Blackwell's, the famous Oxford bookstore, reading books off the shelf and then replacing them, his clothing covered in cigarette ash and assorted stains.

He was a very messy man—he always was, and there are numerous stories of the conditions of domestic disarray in which he lived. Some years ago I visited Williamsburg, Virginia, where I was due to deliver a talk at the College of William and Mary. My hosts were members of the English faculty, and one of them was married to a writer who told me an extraordinary story about Auden. We were in the car, traveling from the airport at which I had arrived, when, knowing of my admiration for Auden, he mentioned that as a teenager in New York he had met the poet. I asked him to tell the story.

He had written poetry, as some teenagers do, but, unlike most teenagers, he had decided to go to the top in seeking an opinion of his work. He wrote to Auden, enclosing some of his work, and Auden wrote back. That, in itself, was a fine thing: many such letters go off into an uncertain future and are never answered. This may be regrettable, but it is at least understandable: some public figures may be overwhelmed by correspondence and find it impossible to reply to all the letters they receive. They should not be judged too harshly for that, perhaps, but those who do reply should certainly be given moral credit.

Auden's reply was encouraging, and the young man was emboldened to send further samples of his work. This led in due course to an invitation to call at Auden's apartment to discuss the work. There was nothing untoward in this invitation, and the meeting consisted of a serious discussion of the poetry that the young man had been writing. But lunch was served amid great domestic squalor, and this gave rise to the story of the Audenesque chocolate pudding encountered by Vera Stravinsky. Mrs. Stravinsky, visiting Auden and Kallman for dinner, went into the bathroom and discovered on top of the cistern a bowl containing an awful brown mess. This she flushed down the toilet, thinking that she was improving the flat's hygiene but only to discover that she had disposed of the chocolate pudding placed there to cool.

The young poet's story tells us about Auden's quiet, but very touching, kindness. Auden helped people. Sometimes this took extraordinary forms: he was kind, for example, to a Canadian burglar who wrote to him from prison. He wrote back, encouraging the burglar in his interest in poetry. (Canada no doubt has its share of burglars, but for some reason there seems something surprising in the concept of a Canadian burglar—something vaguely oxymoronic).

He died in a hotel room in Vienna and was buried in Kirchstetten, the village where he lived and where he was much appreciated and honored. At his funeral, the village band played him to his grave. The funeral of any great artist may be particularly poignant because it is the end of all the beauty he created; that it should come to this—a cluster of friends and relatives, around the resting place, with flowers and the dying notes of a brass band.

Those are the simple, stripped-down facts. They conceal so much: an immensely complex body of work in which there are layers of meaning and reference that could take a lifetime to understand; a noble and generous heart; a courteous and urbane citizen of a troubled century; a man who somehow seems to speak personally to his reader. They conceal a person who might be the best of guides to the inescapable task of being human; who might, if we allow him, really change our lives.

3

A Discovery of Auden

I saw Auden only once. It was in Edinburgh, a short time before his death, at a reading that he gave in the University Lecture Theatre in George Square. I was in my mid-twenties at the time, and I had just taken up my first academic post in Belfast. I was back in Edinburgh for a visit when I stumbled upon a notice announcing that W. H. Auden would read from his work at such-and-such a time on such-and-such a day. I got hold of a ticket and found a seat close to the front.

The poet came in, flanked by members of the committee of the Scottish Society for the Speaking of Verse. The party mounted the stage and introductions were made. Then Auden stood up, and it became evident that the fly-buttons of his trousers were undone. There was an audible gasp from the audience, but Auden seemed unaware of anything untoward or, if he was aware of it, did not care. He began to recite his work, entirely from memory, including "The Fall of Rome" and "Musée des Beaux Arts."

"The Fall of Rome" is a portrait of decline. If Auden was at pains to stress the virtues of the civic sense and the city, he was also aware of how such things can fall apart. In this poem the images of such decline are particularly vivid:

Fantastic grow the evening gowns;
Agents of the Fisc pursue
Absconding tax-defaulters through
The sewers of provincial towns.

Private rites of magic send
The temple prostitutes to sleep;
All the literati keep
An imaginary friend . . .

Caesar's double bed is warm
As an unimportant clerk
Writes I DO NOT LIKE MY WORK
On a pink official form.

Lines like that are memorable; indeed, they can get under one's skin. When I see a picture of a glittering occasion, with fantastic evening gowns, I am sometimes tempted to think of the impermanence of empires; when I encounter a minor bureaucrat—a customs official, perhaps, annotating those largely useless forms that we have to fill in when we cross a border—I wonder whether he or she would not like to write in "I DO NOT LIKE MY WORK." And as for the agents of the Fisc pursuing tax-defaulters through the sewers—that is pure Graham Greene, pure Harry Lime. When I read in the newspapers of the arrest of some financial criminal, I am tempted to imagine that the arrest took place in a sewer, a *paysage moralisé* if ever there was one.

There is a modern term for lines of poetry or song that stick in the mind in this way—a *worm*. Most of us experience these worms from time to time; we hear a snatch of melody and later we hum it repetitively. For me, it tends to be a line of poetry; the line returns again and again until it becomes part of the way I look at things. It may be a line of Auden, or it may be a line from some other poet. Michael Longley, the distinguished Northern Irish poet, once wrote a poem in which he referred to the landscapes of Ireland and of Scotland. There is a line from that poem that comes to me again and again: "I think of Tra-ra-Rossan, Inisheer / Of Harris drenched by horizontal rain." I find that last line very beautiful; Harris is an island in the Outer Hebrides of Scotland. I have a house on the edge of the Hebridean Sea, and it is close to such islands. When I see an island swept by rain, Michael Longley's lines often come back to me, as if they were background music orchestrated for the very scene before me.

I do not mind this in the least—why should one mind? It is rather like having the poet by one's side—ready to point something out, ready to put into words a feeling or impression that would otherwise be fleeting. And I think we need these familiar references. In the past, many people had them from religious liturgy or from exposure to biblical texts—or they picked them up from poetry they had been obliged to learn by rote as children. This is no longer the case, with the result that our stock of metaphor, the range of our vocabulary, contract and language becomes dry and technical—and less morally and imaginatively powerful.

As Auden read these poems, the unmistakable accent, English with an overlay of American, was compelling; the famous face, with its geological catastrophe of lines and crevasses, held the audience. The fact that he was a sartorial disaster, wearing a stained and ash-spattered suit and battered carpet slippers, in no sense detracted from the impact of his words. This was what the audience had come to see and to hear, and it was being delivered.

A short while later he died. I was then back in Belfast and had gone out on a Sunday morning to buy a newspaper. I turned the corner into the street in which I lived and read, on the front page, the headline, AUDEN DIES. The article revealed that Auden had been in a hotel in Vienna and had been found dead by Chester Kallman. Isherwood, it said, was too distraught to make any comment to reporters. I remember thinking: What did they expect? I have never understood why the press feels that it is appropriate to try to interview those in a state of grief.

I walked the rest of the way back home feeling that curious emptiness that can sometimes come after receiving the news of a death. This emptiness can sometimes seem all the greater when you did not know the person who has died, but you admired him or her. Perhaps it increases the poignancy; one has lost a friend one never really had the chance to have. In this case, I felt that a great humane voice had been silenced. I felt a strange sense of loss, as one feels when a personal hero dies. Public people, people we do not actually know but whose lives or work means something to us, become part of our lives. They are like friends, and their death moves us in the same way as does the death of a friend.

I read a great deal of poetry as a child. I had a rambling set of volumes called *Arthur Mee's Children's Encyclopaedia*, my proudest possession, and this had pages of poetry among the articles on famous explorers and the Pyramids of Egypt that such books tended to contain. This started me on poetry, and by the time I was in my teens I had read screeds of Tennyson, Longfellow, and the like, with a smattering of the moderns, including Eliot ("A cold coming we had of it . . .") and Lawrence ("A snake came to my water trough, on a hot, hot day, and I in pyjamas for the heat . . ."). I had, too, a slender paperback of translations of Yevgeny Yevtushenko; I was so proud of the ownership of this book—Russian poetry! And I *owned* it whereas others in my class at school had *no idea* who Yevtushenko was!) For various reasons, Auden had not featured in this; he was obviously far too *outré* for Arthur Mee, and the moralists who edited school textbooks would perhaps have caviled at including a poet who was synonymous with left-wing ideals of the 1930s and the permissive sexual attitudes that went with all that. So by the time I was nineteen, my reading may have included Spender and MacNeice but had embraced little Auden apart from one or two poems of his that I encountered in anthologies. It was in one of the Guinness anthologies, I think, that I first came across "Goodbye to the Mezzogiorno." That was, I think, the first poem that I read of his, and I am not sure if at that point I understood it fully. I had not been to Italy at that stage, and so I did not understand the full contrast, so strikingly portrayed by Auden, between the culture of northern Europe and that of the South of Italy, between northern Protestantism and the relaxed Catholicism of the Mediterranean.

Can Auden be read by young people? I have often wondered which of his poems I should recommend to younger readers and have not always been able to come up with suggestions that will get them started on him. This did not stop my introducing my elder daughter to his work at the age of four, in what, in retrospect, seems an absurd example of the pushy parent hothousing a child. I read her "As I Walked Out" and taught her to recite the first few verses. She appeared to enjoy this, and we still have a film of her sitting on a sofa, wearing a curious red hat, reciting, "As I walked out one evening, walking down Bristol Street, The crowds upon the pavement, Were fields of golden wheat."

Of course it is not with four-year-olds that a proselyte of Auden's work might be concerned; the more appropriate young audience is that aged between, say, sixteen and twenty-something. This group certainly responded to "Funeral Blues" when it was recited by a grieving lover in the film *Four Weddings and a Funeral*:

Stop all the clocks, cut off the telephone,
Prevent the dog from barking with a juicy bone,
Silence the pianos and the muffled drum
Bring out the coffin, let the mourners come.

Let aeroplanes circling overhead
Scribbling on the sky the message He Is Dead,
Put crepe bows round the white necks of the public doves,
Let the traffic policeman wear black cotton gloves.

He was my North, my South, my East and West,
My working week and my Sunday rest,
My noon, my midnight, my talk, my song;
I thought that love would last forever: I was wrong.

The stars are not wanted now: put out every one;
Pack up the moon and dismantle the sun;
Pour away the ocean and sweep up the wood;
For nothing now can ever come to any good.

Auden in general speaks to the more mature mind, but the raw sorrow and sense of loss that this poem conveys spoke to a young audience that had probably never heard of him. And the same might be said of "September 1, 1939," another poem that touched the public imagination so vividly. That poem was photocopied and faxed around New York in the aftermath of the attack on the World Trade towers. I suspect that many of the recipients similarly had never encountered Auden but were profoundly touched by the gentle resignation of many of the lines of that poem. Auden, when encountered for the first time, can touch the heart, can bowl one over, as these opening lines from that poem can certainly do:

I sit in one of the dives
On Fifty-second Street,
Uncertain and afraid
As the clever hopes expire
Of a low, dishonest decade . . .

The dive in question does its best, but its denizens are who they are:

Faces along the bar
Cling to their average day;
The lights must never go out,
The music must always play,
All the conventions conspire
To make this fort assume
The furniture of home;
Lest we should see where we are,
Lost in a haunted wood,
Children afraid of the night
Who have never been happy or good.

Auden has a knack of seeing exactly who we are, and with that self-knowledge comes a very particular benison. I wish that somebody had put a volume of Auden into my hands at the age of fourteen or fifteen. I wish that somebody had been able to explain him to me, to accompany me through a line-by-line exegesis of poems such as "In Memory of Sigmund Freud." What a comfort that would have been; what a release from the very oppression that he talks about in those lines. Most of us, of course, wish for that sort of thing. We think back to our youth and wish that we had had somebody who could have taught us not to worry, could have laid our anxieties to rest, could have relieved us of unnecessary unhappiness.

As it was, my real discovery of Auden came during that time in Belfast, in 1973 and 1974. I remember browsing in the university library and wandering past the poetry shelves. A blue-covered hardback book attracted my attention: *Collected Shorter Poems*, by W. H. Auden, published by Faber and Faber. I borrowed that book and started to read it that afternoon. I was immediately in thrall, in particular to the Freud poem, and I read my way through if not all, then the majority of the poems in that collection before returning it to the library. I had no idea, of course, that I was making the greatest literary discovery of my life. Thereafter there would be no writer who made as profound and lasting an impression on me; no writer whose work I would carry about with me in my suitcase when traveling, as a priest may carry his missal, or a diarist his diary.

We do not always remember the precise circumstances in which we first make an important intellectual encounter. I have many favorite writers, but only in very few cases do I remember how I first came to them. I remember my discovery of Somerset Maugham, whom I first read in my late twenties when I was spending a month at a research institute in Hastings-on-Hudson, in New York. I had resisted Maugham for some reason, in the way in which we sometimes put off reading a particular book or author, not for any good reason but simply, and perversely, because we have decided that we do not read that book or that author. That summer, though, I read *Of Human Bondage* sitting in the porch of the house I was staying in, so far from the London of Maugham's story. I also recall the circumstances of one or two other literary discoveries, of recommendations made by friends, but not in the same detail as I remember this first reading of Auden.

Where we are when we read something can make a difference to how we respond to it. Auden's earlier work is written in response to political and social crisis. In a later chapter I shall return to this theme, but for now I raise it to make the point that reading Auden in troubled circumstances gives his work a particular resonance. When I first started to read Auden I was in Northern Ireland, and it was in the time of the Troubles that began in 1968 and continued until the first years of the twenty-first century. The word *troubles* is a somewhat poetic Irish expression; in reality Ulster was seized by what can only be described as a low-grade civil war. British troops patrolled the streets; the police moved about in armored cars; the sound of exploding bombs was a regular occurrence. At night the city was largely deserted, a northern Beirut, divided into mutually hostile zones. In such an air of crisis, Auden's thirties poetry seemed utterly apt, with its sense of things about to go wrong, of unreason about to be unleashed.

It was not just Auden that I read at the time. That year in Belfast was for me a period of discovery of Irish writing—of Brian Moore, the novelist, whose *Lonely Passion of Miss Judith Hearne* and *The Doctor's Wife* capture so beautifully the atmosphere of middle-class Belfast. I also came across Michael Longley, one of the finest poets of his generation and also the most accomplished interpreter of that special Belfast poetic sensibility. Political crisis lends an edge to poetry—both to its writing and to its reading. Auden was a good companion, then, to the sense of danger that hung over Northern Ireland at that time. He had experienced something infinitely more sinister in his encounter with European fascism, but what he wrote about still seemed to be relevant to times where fear and distrust hung in the air about one. Auden helped; he was exactly that rational voice to which he alludes in his poem to Freud. He said that poetry had nothing to teach us, but he was wrong about that; just as he was self-confessedly wrong in his assessment in "Funeral Blues" that love has no ending.

4

Choice and Quest

One of the pleasures of coming to Auden in one's twenties—as I did—is the strong sense of identification that one can develop with the poet in his early years. In one's twenties one can read what Auden wrote at the same stage in his life, and earlier, and imagine how he felt—because that is how one feels oneself. Yet one sees that there is a later Auden, the Auden at the height of his powers round about the time of his departure for America, and soon thereafter; one then encounters the mature Auden, the Auden of settled views, the religious Auden; and finally the cantankerous and complaining Auden of late middle-age, the Auden who complained about modern manners and carped on about the boredom and vulgarity of a changed world. Here then is a whole life reflected in a body of poetry that changes in its preoccupation and emphasis, mirroring, too, a whole swathe of a turbulent century. It is not impossible to chart development in the life of other writers, but there are few, I feel, whose work reveals so clearly the intellectual history of an age without being tied so closely to the particular as to become dated and irrelevant once the world has moved on. There is, then, in Auden's work a strong sense of biography, even if he generally eschews the sort of personal poetry that one finds, for instance, in the work of Robert Lowell. Lowell's *Notebooks* became a favorite of mine in the late 1970s, but I always felt that in reading these poems I was listening to a poet addressing a circle of friends and contemporaries of whom I knew nothing and would never meet. Auden's friends are present in his poems—often as dedicatees—but any conversation he has with them is not a private one. Auden uses the first-person pronoun sparingly and, even when he does, the *I* transcends the purely personal and sounds more like a *we* that naturally and courteously includes the reader. Even at his most intimate, in his gravely beautiful "Lullaby," we know that the poet was there and that these, or something like these, must have been his thoughts, and yet he speaks for all of us who have been vouchsafed a personal vision of Eros.

It is sometimes said that writers give themselves away every third sentence, no matter how much they protest their detachment. Small wonder, then, that readers as well as critics should believe that their appreciation of a work might be aided by an understanding of its author. Some authors dislike this intensely; the historical novelist Patrick O'Brian once commented on what he described as the effrontery of a journalist who asked him his age. Auden felt that his private life was his own affair even if at times his poems are extremely revealing of the moral and psychological growth of their author. Auden was at pains to stress that his poems should be judged as creations in themselves and not as an outcrop of the poet's personal life. If such a wish was unlikely to be honored in the first half of the last century, how much more unlikely would it be in an age of deconstruction and persistent intrusion.

The early Auden is rich and rewarding, as full as any young man can be of determination to find a way through life, as excited as any of us feel at the outset of adult life. Auden liked to obscure the context in which his poems were written by ignoring, or indeed confusing, chronology, but wherever the early poems are placed in a collection, they will stand out for the strength and vividness of their imagery. This is poetry that engages strongly with landscape—with roads and cliffs and lead mines; it is the poetry of a young man looking at his world and trying to see what lies beneath it. It also shows the beginning of the spiritual quest that was to feature in all his work: the young Auden is searching for the way that will lead him through life—he is looking for a purpose, for a role that will enable him to live honestly and to heal the rift both between man and nature and between the contradictory aspects of the poet's personality.

The sense of quest in Auden's life led him to engage in a series of adventures in which he became for a time the man of action that he realized he never was. The scholar poet is not the hero athlete—and usually knows it—but may try to be. I find Auden's life absorbing because it is very unlike the life of those poets who appear to have done nothing but frequent academia. How can one write convincingly of life if one has seen only so small a slice of it? Hemingway asked that question and went off to preclude its application to him by hunting and deep-sea fishing, all fueled by copious quantities of whisky. Auden spoke in his earlier poems of the truly strong man but well understood that one did not become truly strong by doing the sort of things recommended by Hemingway. Rather, he traveled; first to Berlin, where he spent a great deal of time catching up on sexual opportunities harder to encounter in the more prudish climate of England. Berlin was all about sexual freedom, but it was also about politicization, and by the time he returned to England, his previously proclaimed views on the separation of poetry and politics had changed. Then there was the trip to Iceland he did with Louis MacNeice, the trip to Spain during the Civil War, and the journey to China to investigate the conflict with Japan. These were not the actions of a man who intended to live his life in a literary ivory tower; these were the actions of a man who was struggling with a central moral question that most of us face: to what extent should we seek private peace or follow public duty? The world is a vale of tears and always has been. We may withdraw from it and cultivate a private garden of civility and the arts—a temptation that is often strong; or we may face up to uncomfortable realities and work to bring about justice in society. Auden's life and example illustrates the struggle between these two options; significantly, it offers comfort to us whichever way our choice may lead us.

5

The Poet as Voyager

The work that emerged from these trips is varied and shows both the strengths and flaws in Auden's poetry. The connecting theme, though, is that of the *journey*, and it is not a journey undertaken for diversion or relaxation, as so many of our journeys now are. Auden traveled as part of his quest; the trip to Berlin was an escape from sexual repressiveness in England and an exploration of that part of his nature; the trip to Iceland seems to have been motivated by a desire to get away from Europe and its problems, to travel back in *time*, in a sense; the trips to Spain and China were part of a program of progressively more intense political involvement.

The Iceland trip was a mixture of despair, discomfort, insight, and sheer farce. Auden must have been a curious sight, in the strange outfit he chose for the riding part of the trip—an outfit built up on a base of pyjamas and culminating, after various jerseys, in a layer of yellow oilskin. And it is hard not to laugh at the idea of Auden and MacNeice, in the dying days of the trip, being entertained by the director of what was then known as a lunatic asylum and being invited to spend the night in the hospital. The doctor, having no common language with them, spoke to the two poets in Latin. A similarly surreal anecdote comes from the Chinese trip that Auden was later to embark upon with Christopher Isherwood. On this trip they found themselves having tea with Madam Chiang Kai-shek, who asked them if poets like cake. "I thought they preferred only spiritual food," she said.

Letters from Iceland is one of Auden's oddest books. It belongs to that comparatively rare genre, the epistolary travel book, and is very loosely organized, foretelling, in parts, the potpourri of curious facts that is his commonplace book, *A Certain World*. Auden acquired a great deal of knowledge about Iceland in the time he was there, and much of it is delightfully arcane. The professional travel writer, Auden felt, was a serious creature, obliged by the expectations of the reader to give an informative account of history and geography; Auden and MacNeice, by contrast, waffled, interspersing letters to friends with poems, epistolary and otherwise. The strange facts included are very strange; if Auden went there to escape the constraints of the life he was leading and to find an alternative to European concerns, then he was amply rewarded.

The finest poem in the book is one that in my view reveals Auden's imagery at its most lyrically powerful. I have a house in Argyll, a remote part of Scotland, where the Atlantic comes sweeping up against a coast of islands. When I look out to sea there, Auden's hauntingly beautiful words often come to me, as a snatch of song or a passage of music may be associated with some familiar and much-loved place:

And the traveller hopes: 'Let me be far from any
Physician'; and the ports have names for the sea;
The citiless, the corroding, the sorrow;
And North means to all: 'Reject!'

And the great plains are for ever where the cold fish
  is hunted,

And everywhere; the light birds flicker and flaunt;
Under the scolding flag the lover
Of islands may see at last

Faintly, his limited hope . . .

These are exquisite lines, quintessentially Audenesque. They surprise and entrance, and one can see the great plains of the sea and the scolding flag fluttering on the ship as the islands come into sight. And yet they reveal one of Auden's great faults: that of falling in love with words irrespective of their meaning. The reader is likely to wonder why any traveler would wish to be far from a physician; far from crowds, yes; far from bureaucrats or importuning traders, yes; but far from a physician? Unless, of course, the physician stands for all that is overly fussy and cosseting in modern society; in which case we would want him or her absent in order to experience *danger*. The answer, though, is probably more prosaic: hoping to be far from a physician is a way of saying that you hope you don't fall ill; expressing the thought so simply, however, does not sound very poetic.

And then we come to that famous and troubling phrase, "and the ports have names for the sea." As Auden reveals in a letter, he meant to write *poets* but ports is what was printed. He could have changed the typographical error, but he felt that this sounded better and the mistake was kept. What this demonstrates is a willingness to sacrifice meaning to sound, a tendency that means that some of Auden's lines end up being either obscure to the point of being nonsensical, or just plain wrong. This is pointed out with some delight by the somewhat acerbic critic, A. L. Rowse, who takes Auden to task for saying things that are not true just because he likes the sound of the words.

The fact that the ports had names for the sea reveals another of Auden's curious traits— that of personalizing the inanimate. Unlike the choosing of words for effect, this is a harmless habit; indeed I feel that it adds substantially to the charm and impact of Auden's work. Only when he allows History to speak does it appear at all sinister—but there are many others, entire movements, that had done that with History. The line "Perhaps the roses really want to grow," taken from "If I Could Tell You," is an example of this inclination to attribute human feelings to inanimate objects, nonhuman beings, or natural forces. "Come says the wind" is another, as is the inferring, in "Streams," of playful moods in water. This personalization does more than serve the poet's rhetorical purpose; it reminds us that Auden felt keenly our separation from nature and the need to become one with it again.

6

Politics and Sex

Auden went to Spain in 1937 because it was a central concern of the British literary Left and he wanted to see at firsthand what he felt he had to write about. Spain for many in the thirties was a defining moment in the struggle against fascism, and there were numerous volunteers who joined the International Brigade in its support of the Republican government. Auden did not go to fight, but he was still involved to the extent of broadcasting propaganda for the government. He did not regard the trip as particularly successful, but it did bring forth one of his most controversial poems, "Spain," a poem that was later to be heavily criticized—most notably by George Orwell—and that he later suppressed on the grounds of its meretricious nature. Auden was refreshingly honest about his work. Few writers are prepared to decry what they have written; they may be prepared to consign manuscripts to the bottom drawer, or, if the offending work has been published, they may hope that it will be forgotten, but it is usual for them to disown them publicly or, as in Auden's case, to pronounce that what they have written is pure lies.

At one level "Spain" is not much more than a piece of political propaganda—the sort of poem that an engaged poet of the Left might offer as a contribution to the struggle. As such it might be disregarded, other than as a historical curiosity: posturing of any sort destroys the spirit of honesty that should lie at poetry's heart. But at another level, "Spain" is about choice and responsibility—themes that run deep in Auden's work and that occur in this poem, even they are overshadowed by the poem's broader context and ramifications. These are great and important issues, and they save the poem from train wreck.

But first, the political dimension. Auden's politics at the time were in no way exceptional. The thirties—described by Auden with such devastating force in "September 1, 1939," as a "low dishonest decade," were years in which Europe drifted into what was probably the greatest moral disaster of its history: aggressive fascism. There have been other European evils: communism, for all its professed concern with economic injustice, plumbed depths of cruelty every bit as inventive as those revealed by fascism. Fascism, however, as practiced in Germany, Spain, and Italy was egregiously wicked, its victims ultimately to be counted in their millions. For many of Auden's generation, who had yet to see Stalin play his hand, the choice seemed to be between those who were prepared to combat fascism most directly—and that moral high ground was claimed most vociferously by socialists and communists—and those who would ignore or appease the threat. Bourgeois democracies might have disapproved of the strutting of dictators but seemed to have little stomach for the fight. And it was a common view among intellectuals of the time that these societies were rotten anyway, uninterested in justice for the common man, only wishing to perpetrate the comfortable arrangements they provided for their propertied classes.

Of course Auden would be opposed to what he saw as these stuffy and creaking societies. What young man, brought up in the stifling atmosphere of the English upper middle class, with its fixation on social standing, could do anything—

if he thought about things at all—other than rebel? And how romantic would seem the world of the real working man—how authentic too. Communism beckoned precisely because it was all about those who were outside that tradition: to join the ranks of those fighting for the working man was an act of cleansing, a rejection of one's uncomfortable past.

Auden's discomfort with the society into which he had been born must have been a major factor in his alignment with the Left. It is possible to reach a political position on the basis of a rational and considered examination of the available alternatives, but for many of us there are less obvious factors that may have a major influence on our social and political choices. One of these is sexuality, a factor that it seems reasonable to assume influenced Auden's political and social attitudes, especially in his early years.

Auden was born into an England in which homosexuality was not officially tolerated. The trial of Oscar Wilde, which rocked late Victorian society, demonstrated that although sexually unconventional behavior was winked at and, in some circumstances, admired, actual homosexual affairs were extremely dangerous.

The authorities could be brutal and would not hesitate to prosecute and imprison men who were found to have engaged in sexual activity with other men; lesbians were altogether more fortunate, as the criminal law largely ignored them. One suggested explanation for this double standard was Queen Victoria's disbelief that lesbianism actually existed, and hence its removal from the sexual offenses legislation to which she was asked to give her assent. Auden was educated at a single-sex private school (or public school, as they are perversely called in Britain). The culture of such schools was, not surprisingly, one that encouraged—even if unintentionally—homosexuality while at the same time energetically disapproving of it, warning boys against its insidious ways. And yet the British public school system kept boys and young men apart from girls, engendering a hypocritical, repressive attitude to sexuality in which sex with other boys and men was often the only available outlet. Auden grew up in such a world. (So, too, did Anthony Blunt, the art historian and spy, who probably learned at boarding school, Marlborough College, how to dissemble and use sex as a weapon; who learned, as well, to hate the

Establishment and its brutality; who learned, in other words, all about oppression and treachery.)

A gay man in those circumstances was condemned to a tragic psychic bifurcation between what he was and what he was expected or needed to be. If he was honest with himself he might confront and admit to his sexual orientation, but that then meant that he must admit to being, in the eyes of society at large, a criminal or at least a potential criminal. Such a position could easily result in self-hatred, and it could also result in feeling detached from the culture that so clearly rejects one. It would be surprising, then, if the young Auden had not felt himself an outsider, eager to find a haven in more tolerant, accepting political circles. The moral certainties of the Left are comfortable for those who feel themselves rejected, and a sexual nonconformist might well find such circles welcoming.

Those moral certainties also offer a new beginning: the old self can be replaced by a shining new you. It is not surprising that Auden should have identified with the Left at that stage in his life. Yet even if there was a psychological predisposition to adopting the stance of the rebel—the eternal intelligent schoolboy in revolt against the dim-witted school authorities—there was still a profound moral impulse behind this choice. "Spain" reveals this in the lines that constitute the central argument of this striking, allegorical poem:

What's your proposal? To build the just city? I will.
I agree. Or is it the suicide pact, the romantic
Death? Very well, I accept, for
I am your choice, your decision. Yes, I am Spain.

Even if a desire that the right side should win prompted Auden to write "Spain," the poem strays into dangerous territory in its claim to speak for history. The offending lines that attracted the attention of George Orwell were these: "Today the deliberate increases in the chances of death / The conscious acceptance of guilt in the necessary murder." Orwell was appalled at what he saw as an acceptance by the intelligentsia of killing as a means to a political end. Although he later changed these lines, Auden felt that Orwell had been unjust in this criticism; he had not intended to justify political murder—he had intended, rather, to express the difficulties that a feeling person must have when he engages in the just war.

The poem's finale is even more difficult. If, at the end of the day, the struggle for justice fails, then we arrive in a place of despair. Surveying our failure is History, and "History to the defeated / May say Alas but cannot help or pardon." Auden was embarrassed to have espoused such a view, later suggesting that "to say this is to equate goodness with success," a position he described as a "wicked doctrine." As John Fuller has pointed out, though, if it means that History is merely a random collection of events, with no real pattern behind it, then one can readily see a defensible point in the original remark. History does not dictate what *is to* happen, even if it helps us to assess probable outcomes: it explains what *has* happened. But this, although interesting, does not change the fact that Auden himself knew what he meant when he wrote those lines and disowned that meaning—the fact that the lines can be given an innocent interpretation is surely neither here nor there.

The emphasis on choice in "Spain" is far more important and imparts to the poem its continuing value, even if shame prompted Auden to remove it from the canon. In going to Spain, Auden made the choice to engage in the great political issue of his time. He did not see himself as a fighter, but at least he committed himself in a way that seemed right for him. He wanted to bridge the gap between the thinker who can see evil in the world and the doer who tackles it. And for many of us, even if we do not see ourselves as political and social thinkers, that is still a problematic issue. What can we do to combat those things that we see as hostile to human flourishing? How do we tackle injustice and wrong in our own times?

Auden answers that in two ways. The first answer is in his life. If we look at Auden's life we can see a struggle with the whole idea of engagement: in his earlier years he responded to the demands of his time; he bore witness—and each of us can do the same, even if we do it on a more modest scale than he did. Later, of course, his position changed, and he became more of an observer than a participant—but that, surely, is true of all of us, or at least true of all except those few who refuse to leave the party at a seemly time. The second answer is to be found in the poems themselves. Auden helps us to respond to the world, as any good poet will do, and shows us how a life embedded in a culture may find in that culture the things that sustain us and point us in the direction of good choices. Auden, like any great poet or any great artist, for that matter, helps us to live.

7

If I Could Tell You I Would Let You Know

Choice and responsibility are in fact two of the great themes in Auden's earlier work. Responsibility cannot exist without choice: Aristotle emphasized that in his theory of moral responsibility, and the linkage between the two has remained at the heart of philosophical treatments of accountability since then. If I cannot do otherwise, if I have no choice, then I cannot be held responsible for what I do. We do not blame an automaton for his acts because there they do not represent any volition on his part; nor do we generally blame (although some might) those who act at the point of a gun. Those are extreme cases: there are many cases where the issue is less clear-cut and where it is consequently more difficult to determine the extent of individual responsibility.

A large part of my academic career was concerned with issues of responsibility for actions in the context of theories of criminal responsibility. I started off this fairly long tussle with the subject with a doctoral thesis on the subject of the criminal liability of those who committed crimes under duress. My interest in this was triggered at about the same time that I began to read Auden, although it was not Auden who led me to the subject in the first place. That was in Belfast, when I was working at the university there, and came across a case of a man who had been obliged to drive an IRA hit-team on an assassination mission. The driver knew that if he failed to comply with the team's orders he would be shot; he complied and was subsequently charged with being an accessory to the murder they committed.

The question of the liability of those who take another's life to save their own skin is a well-rehearsed one in criminal jurisprudence. Generations of law students have cut their teeth on the extraordinary criminal cases in which this issue has arisen—notably the Victorian cause célèbre of Dudley and Stephens, two shipwrecked sailors who killed and ate the cabin boy to stave off starvation. Such legal decisions as there have been in this area tend to exclude any excusing those who kill to save themselves—a principle endorsed at Nuremberg in the trials of war criminals. One can readily understand all that, but at a more prosaic level, in relation to ordinary wrongdoing, it is hard to ignore the extent to which our actions are the result of influences over which we have never had any real control. We are what we are because we are who we are, and who we are is usually not the result of choice on our part but is the result of factors outside our control. These include the fact of birth: in so many cases the bed in which one is born determines well nigh every major aspect our lives—our views, our chances, our careers. We may create ourselves to some extent—life would be bleak if we had no chance to do that—but the shape of our life is often determined by external factors such as geography and the sheer accident of being born into a particular society at a particular time.

My personal reflections over the years of the notion of responsibility seemed to lead me into an uncomfortably determinist position. The more I thought about it, the more I realized that the territory of real responsibility—those things for which we had to shoulder complete blame—was small indeed. Auden's insights into this issue were useful, as indeed he was useful on so many matters. One particularly resonant statement of this occurs in "September 1, 1939," that hauntingly beautiful poem to which I find myself frequently returning, in spite of what Auden himself thought of it. Auden is talking about Germany, and about what went wrong:

> Accurate scholarship can
> Unearth the whole offence
> From Luther until now
> That has driven a culture mad,
> Find what occurred at Linz,
> What huge imago made
> A psychopathic god:
> I and the public know
> What all schoolchildren learn,
> Those to whom evil is done
> Do evil in return.

This stanza is typical of the intellectual density of Auden's poetry: a few lines pack in a vast amount of meaning, whole hinterlands of scholarship and understanding. Germany's behavior is not random, he suggests: it can be explained by an understanding of the events that have shaped German culture since Luther and the beginning of Protestantism set off the split between feeling and intellect. This wound, as Auden thought of it, preoccupied him: we need, he thought, to restore our sense of identification with nature, with our past, with ourselves. This message, of course, will not sound strange to contemporary ears: it is what the Green movement has been preaching and continues to preach.

From Luther we move to Hitler, and to his hometown of Linz. The mention of what occurred in Linz is probably a reference to the events of Hitler's childhood rather than to the later scenes of enthusiastic welcoming of the *Anschluss*. Auden's view of Hitler as a psychopath will hardly be controversial; but even if some more complicated psychopathology was present, the issue is: what produces a personality like Hitler's? An unhappy childhood? Neuro-anatomical abnormality? The willing choice of evil? Auden has a tendency to come up with the neat explanation, particularly if it can be made to sound good. This is not necessarily a fault in poetry, which needs the aphorism—indeed it would be difficult to imagine how a poet might make anything of the more subtle, nuanced explanation of reality: the pithy expression rarely admits of qualification. And here the poet sides with that approach. Auden and the public do not need to be told of Germany's intellectual history or of Hitler's pathological upbringing; they *know* that if you treat somebody badly, he or she in turn behaves badly. It is not a sophisticated adage, but it is one that is constantly being proved true.

"Those to whom evil is done / Do evil in return": this has the ring of nursery wisdom to it—the sort of adage that one encounters, or used to encounter, in a child's picture book or as the carefully worked text of a Victorian sampler. (I remember a teacup from my boyhood on which the words "Say not always what you know but always know what you say" were imprinted around the rim. We rarely forget these sayings of childhood, and their continuing power must be immense.) Nursery references crop up in a number of Auden's poems, where there are allusions to the safe world of childhood and occasionally, as in "As I Walked Out," to the characters of that world who may not behave as they are expected to. Jack, for example, is treated well by the Giant, and Jill, it turns out, is sexually voracious. Similarly in "Nursery Rhyme" the sinister nature of many of these rhymes is gleefully explored. The world of the nursery rhyme is turned upside down: cheerful kings made toffee on their stoves but only until the everything went wrong—the loaves rotted, woolly bears began to pursue the spotted dogs, our bowls of milk became full of drowning frogs, and so on.

The gist of that stanza in "September 1, 1939," is that our disposition will be, in some measure, the result of our upbringing. There is hardly anything earth-shattering in this observation—we often reflect on that when we contemplate the behavior of others. But I am not sure that we are prepared to think through the consequences of this view when it comes to determining responsibility and allocating blame. The youth from a deprived background, brought up in a climate of disregard for the law, will not surprise us when he conforms to expectations and commits a crime. But that is often as far as our understanding goes: we may be very unwilling to take that into account in determining blame. Had he been given more opportunities, had he had a father to control him, then he might not have done what he did. Had Hitler been born into a stable and loving home, then he might not have done what he did. Yes, but does that relieve him of responsibility for what he did? The answer must surely be no: nothing excuses that. But what about lesser tyrants? What about the doers of smaller acts of cruelty, minor malefactors, who might well not have acted as they did if only they had experienced human love in more generous quantities? As for evil, can that be solved—or at least understood—by understanding what psychological factors lie behind it? Auden's view on this changed between the 1930s and 1940s, as they did on a number of issues, and his experience of this change helps us, perhaps, in our own confrontation with evil in its contemporary, though ultimately very familiar, forms. One wonders where Auden would find evil in our own twenty-first century world: possibly in the murderous fanaticism of the jihadists, in the ruthlessness of the drug-trafficking barons of Mexico and Colombia; in the child pornographers of the Internet. And how exactly should we deal with it, whatever its causes?

Understanding helps us deal with most threats, and seeking to understand must be our first response to evil, just as it is to anything else with which we have to deal. But there will be limits to our understanding, as Auden points out in "If I Could Tell You." Some things, we come to learn, just *are*.

"If I Could Tell You" is one of the more musical of Auden's poems, written in the form of a villanelle. It is also one of his more enigmatic works, with lines that demonstrate Auden's consummate ability to create arresting imagery that proves unexpectedly difficult to interpret. We read the line and it seems so easy, so true. And then we ask ourselves exactly what it means, and our earlier assumption of understanding begins to look much weaker.

The refrain throughout the poem is that time will say nothing but I told you so. This answer will be given by time no matter what surprising events occur:

> If we should weep when clowns put on their show,
> If we should stumble when musicians play,
> Time will say nothing but I told you so . . .
>
> The winds must come from somewhere when they
>   blow,
> There must be reasons why the leaves decay;
> Time will say nothing but I told you so.

These two stanzas contain two of the most entrancing lines in Auden's entire opus. "If we should weep when clowns put on their show" is a line that is itself surely enough to make one weep. And then "The winds must come from somewhere when they blow" is deeply evocative.

Who among us has not felt the wind on our skin and been in some way transported?

Time, though, has no explanations other than the shrugged "I told you so." This must be because the puzzling or contradictory things that occur in our world are beyond explanation by any overarching force or figure, including Time, who, in one view, presides over our human affairs. This poem invokes the image of Time in Poussin's magnificent painting *Dance to the Music of Time*: Time, in his chariot, rides past on a sea of cloud while below him the figures engage in dance. Of course such a figure is not going to descend to our level to explain these mysteries; he is well above all that.

8

What Freud Meant

How then are we to understand our nature? Like many of his generation, Auden at one point placed great store by the claims of Freudian psychology, even if he believed that Freud was too accepting of conventional morality: if we can understand ourselves and the dynamics of our behavior, then we may improve our ways. In the heyday of Freudianism many people put their faith in that, and some still do. Today the climate is rather different, and the almost religious nature of the Freudian movement has been weakened by mockery and doubt voiced from both within and without. This has led to the rejection of psychoanalysis's claims to be a panacea for human suffering, even if the influence of Freud on twentieth-century thought remains massive, and even if there are many who feel, with good reason, that they have been helped by psychoanalysis.

It was Auden's poem "In Memory of Sigmund Freud" that first inspired me to explore Freudian literature, a body of literature that has continued to give me pleasure ever since. The poem belongs to the period immediately after Auden had gone to live in the United States, the same period that saw the composition of his other great encomium, "In Memory of W. B. Yeats." From the technical point of view, it has several features that make it exceptional: it is a poem of mourning, a public poem delivered as a eulogy to a well-known figure, but it is also an example of the syllabic verse that Auden came to prefer for his later major poems. It is the content, though, that makes this poem so memorable. Freud's interests and work were wide-ranging; this poem succeeds in capturing the salient features of this complex body of work, distilling them in a way that induces in the reader a "well exactly" reaction. It is not a critical assessment, though, but a eulogy for one who represented the antithesis of the dark forces of the time. Unlike many of Auden's earlier poems, it bears no false hope:

Freud shows us the way, he says, but there is no guarantee that his message will triumph.

Freud, says Auden, "wasn't clever at all: he merely told / The unhappy Present to recite the Past / Like a poetry lesson . . . ." The view that Freud was not clever is questionable; he was hardly dull. He certainly did not invent the concept of the subconscious—in my library I have a book that sets out in laborious detail the mentions of the unconscious mind before Freud wrote about it. But the whole point about some really clever thinkers is that the ideas they propound are so self-evidently true that they seem almost mundane. Freud was one such: his exposition of the function of dreams is so convincing, so obvious, that we might conclude that it is a long-established truism. Yet it amounted to a profoundly important insight.

And the same is true of the reciting of the Past by the unhappy Present. Freud's insistence on the importance of allowing the past to surface through analysis is, in a way, no different from the fundamental human recognition that talking to a friend about a problem helps. That, after all, is what we have always done with our friends; the process of talking allows anxieties to emerge, and as this happens we see the dimensions of the problem that has been troubling us. This is effectively the famous "talking cure" that psychoanalysis offers its adherents.

I remain agnostic as to the helpfulness of psychoanalysis. Many decry it, arguing that it its suppositions are unscientific and unprovable. Some go further and argue that the entire psychoanalytical movement has become an elaborate, quasi-religious indulgence, calculated to ensnare unhappy people in a lengthy encounter with an expensive analyst. Certainly an outsider looking at the relationship between analyst and analysand may find instances of what seem like unhelpful dependence. I remember some years ago being in Casablanca and finding my way to a bookshop. Bookshops in Arab countries seem to be, alas, few and far between—a result, perhaps, of the extent to which Arab societies have fallen behind others in literacy and learning; a tragedy, really, in view of their earlier intellectual distinction. This bookshop in Casablanca had a down-at-heel look to it, a thousand miles from the stimulating and exciting bookshops that one might expect to find in a city of comparable size elsewhere. There was a handful of books in English; the majority were in either Arabic or French. I was in no position to judge the Arabic offerings but was able to look at the French selection, which was an odd mixture. One of the titles caught my eye: a history of psychoanalysis in the Land of Saints—the Land of Saints being Morocco.

This book was irresistible. It is a mistake not to buy books as unlikely as that; I once spotted a large tome on monastic sign language in a used bookstore in Toronto but caviled at the outrageous price. Returning to Scotland, I regretted my failure to buy the book: of course I would have loved to have had it, with its lengthy photographic section showing Trappist monks signing their various messages: "The Abbot says that bell must be rung. . . . We must plant potatoes again this year." That sort of thing.

I returned to Toronto the following year and made my way to the bookstore in question. Going up to the desk, I asked the proprietor whether by any chance—and I said I knew it was a remote one—they had in stock a book on the sign language of monks. He looked at me in astonishment that shortly became delight. "As it happens," he began . . . .

I was not going to make the same mistake with the history of psychoanalysis in Morocco. I bought the book and read it on my return to Scotland. The author, a Moroccan doctor who had trained in psychoanalysis abroad, had returned to his native land in the hope of establishing a psychoanalytical training scheme there. Unfortunately Morocco proved to be stony ground for the theories of Freud, and the doctor remained the only psychoanalyst in the country. In the course of relating this melancholy story, he revealed that there had been a small circle of psychoanalysts in Casablanca after the Second World War. These had been effectively forced out of France on Liberation; they were unpopular because they were thought to have been Vichy collaborators. They chose exile in Morocco rather than ostracism in France—and so did their patients, who accompanied them in this exile. They were all getting on in years and eventually the psychoanalysts died, as did their patients. The patients are buried *next to their analysts*.

The polar opposite of Freud's unpopularity in Morocco is his reception in Argentina. Alongside that discouraging volume on Morocco in my library is a much more upbeat work, *Freud on the Pampas*, a book that sets out the extraordinary enthusiasm for psychoanalysis that is to be found in Argentina. I first became aware of this in an article published in the now defunct review *Encounter*, which described the Freudian quarter in Buenos Aires with its Café Sigi, at the tables of which the talk would not be of football or politics but of neuroses and transference and the like.

For many years I nursed a desire to visit this unlikely quarter, but it was not until I found myself spending a few weeks in Montevideo that the opportunity arose to make a pilgrimage to Buenos Aires for this purpose. I arranged a series of meetings in advance with prominent Argentinean psychoanalysts and also set up a visit to the famous Café Sigi. There is always a possibility, of course, that the reality behind a dream will be disappointing; this did not happen in this case. Everything was as I had been led to believe it would be. Yes, virtually everybody who could afford it underwent psychoanalysis; yes, there was a street with numerous door-plates revealing the presence of a psychoanalytical studio; yes, there were bookshops devoted entirely to Freudian—and Lacanian—literature.

The explanation behind this enthusiasm is relatively prosaic. A popular newspaper some fifty years ago introduced a dream analysis column to which readers could write and have their dreams interpreted by the resident analyst. This proved to be very popular and provoked great public interest. At the same time the teaching of psychology in the Argentinean universities began to take on a Freudian note. On these foundations—both popular and academic—the whole edifice of Argentinean psychoanalysis was built.

During the period of military rule, psychoanalysis was unpopular with the generals, who suppressed both its teaching and its practice. Auden's lines come to mind here:

> No wonder the ancient cultures of conceit
> In his technique of unsettlement foresaw
> The fall of princes, the collapse of
> Their lucrative patterns of frustration . . .

Psychoanalysis liberates us from the oppressive judgments of others, Auden points out; it makes us

> able to approach the future as a friend
> without a wardrobe of excuses, without
> a set mask of rectitude or an
> embarrassing over-familiar gesture.

This idea is returned to later in the poem where, in extraordinarily moving lines, he talks about the liberating effect of analysis reaching out to touch

> the child, unlucky in his little State,
> some hearth where freedom is excluded,
> a hive whose honey is fear and worry,
> feels calmer now and somehow assured of escape . . .

"In Memory of Sigmund Freud" gives full credit to Freud for developing the liberating doctrines that allow us to come to terms with our past, to see it for what it is, and not be frightened or oppressed by it. When I read this poem, though, I feel that I recognize Auden in all of this, and that although this poem is about Freud it is also very much about Auden himself, who does all those things too. Freud was a healer, and so was Auden. If Freud said "Don't worry, everything will be all right as long as you understand what has happened," then Auden's message is very much the same. Both throw light on dark corners—the dark furniture of the mind—and show us that the shapes are threatening only because we allow them to be; and after all, they are only shapes.

Toward the end of the poem, Auden returns to one of his most important themes—that of repairing the tragic division in our lives, of making us whole again:

While, as they lie in the grass of our neglect,
So many long-forgotten objects
Revealed by his undisclosed shining
Are returned to us and made precious again;
Games we thought we must drop as we grew up,
Little noises we dared not laugh at,
Faces we made when no one was looking.
But he wishes us more than this. To be free
Is often to be lonely. He would unite
The unequal moieties fractured
By our own well-meaning sense of justice
Would restore to the larger the wit and will
The smaller possess but can only use
For arid disputes, would give back to
The son the mother's richness of feeling . . .

9

A Vision of Agape

It was a summer evening, in June, and I was on my way to a speaking engagement in Perthshire, a part of Scotland that I have always loved for the beauty of its hills and glens. The longest day was only a week or so away, which meant that at that latitude it would barely be dark at midnight. And that evening the light was gentle; not the tired light of a hot day, but that bluish evening light of a day on which the temperature has never really reached the point where one might take off one's jacket and roll up one's sleeves. The invitation had been outstanding for over a year as it had been difficult to find a date that suited both me and the organizers of the event. Now our diaries had coincided and I was shortly to address a gathering of the Friends of the Inerpeffray

Library, one of the oldest libraries in Scotland, having been set up in the seventeenth century by a local landowner of intellectual tastes.

The library lay at the end of a Roman road, surrounded by fields in which wheat and barley were yet to ripen—lush green paddocks half-hidden by unruly hedgerows. Rioting nettles, clumps of blackthorn and rowan, wide-leafed docken grew along the side of the road until suddenly we reached an old schoolhouse and an ancient graveyard of weathered gray stones. The organizers appeared and introduced themselves, and I was taken to see the library before the guests arrived.

Belief in the word can assume the qualities of a religious faith. At the time when Lord Drummond built this place to house his precious collection of books, Scotland was prone to outbreaks of lawlessness and fierce local enmities. The lives of many were lived under the heel of powerful local clan chiefs who administered rough justice. Life was hard in every respect: this was not the rich landscape of settled England—Highland Scotland was a place in which people scraped a living and more often than not went to bed hungry.

It was a place of strong religious views. The Scottish Reformation was late but had been passionate and had brought with it a commitment to the setting up of a school in every parish. What later came to be seen as a strong Scottish commitment to education had its roots in the late sixteenth and early seventeenth centuries. Books were the instruments of truth. Books were the means by which the poor could free themselves of what Auden once described as "the suffering to which they are fairly accustomed." This attitude toward books has stubbornly survived in Scotland, mirroring, perhaps, the Irish attitude to music: both are consolations that will, in their individual way, always see one through.

My talk was preceded by a reception. This was held outside the converted ancient church that the library used for its meetings. A couple of open-sided tents had been erected under which drinks and snacks were prepared, and people milled about, chatting in the benign evening sunlight. In a country such as Scotland, where raw Atlantic weather blows over the land with little regard to season, a sunlit evening in which the air is still lifts the spirits. This lightening was very much in evidence in the atmosphere of the gathering: it seemed as if everybody present was an old friend, seizing the chance to catch up with one another.

I then experienced a feeling of extraordinary calm, of something that must have been joy. It was fleeting, lasting only for a minute or two, but it was unmistakable. We all have such moments in our lives, and there is no telling when they will occur. For a short time we are somehow transported into another form of consciousness, until it comes to an end: we are distracted; somebody says something, a visitor comes to the door (as happened to Coleridge, when that "person from Porlock" interrupted the writing of his visionary poem "Kubla Khan")—and the insight evaporates. But we know that for a short time we have seen something about the world that we do not normally see. I suddenly understood that I loved the people present in that small enclosure. I had come from Edinburgh feeling that the evening would be a chore, and now I stood on the grass and realized how grudging, how churlish that attitude had been.

"A summer night," I said to myself.

Auden wrote "A Summer Night" in 1933, and it was published in the BBC's magazine, *The Listener*, the following year. It was at an important stage in his development as a poet and as a man. In

the very early 1930s Auden had been flirting
with Marxism, although he had not joined the
Communist Party. The attraction that communism exerted upon him perhaps lay not only
in its concern for the downtrodden, but in the
fact that it provided a home—a solution to the
problems of the world and possibly to one's own
immediate difficulties. Arthur Koestler's account
of his own joining of the party is enlightening:
he had taken part in a game of poker at which
he lost heavily and had then gone on a drinking
spree. The weather had changed and he discovered that the engine of his newly mended car
had been destroyed by the freezing of the water in the radiator. He then found himself in the
bed of a woman he did not really like. In such
circumstances, guilt combined with a feeling
of wretchedness made radical action necessary,
and this came in the form of signing up for the
Communist Party.

Auden found no such solution. Membership
in the Communist Party, as he had already rec-
ognized, was simply not authentic to him, and
although there were political poems in the first
years of that decade, by the time he wrote "A
Summer Night" he was embarking on a far more
personal, less politically engaged course. The

emphasis now shifts to the lyrical, and the writing from 1933 onward of a series of sonnets concerned with broad ideas and themes—landscape, history, and love. From the politically engaged younger poet, looked up to for political leadership within a circle of radical figures, is now beginning to emerge the poet whose work will appeal to a wider audience.

He wrote this poem while he was teaching at the Downs School in the Malvern Hills. This was a boarding school, and it was common for some of the boys to take their beds out into the orchard in the warmer weather and sleep under the stars. Sleeping outside in England is to court a soaking, but if it rained, tarpaulins would be erected over the beds for shelter. Auden decided to follow suit, moving his bed outside and using a large umbrella to shelter himself should the weather turn wet. Sometimes this shelter would be shared by geese, which provides us with a lovely picture of the gangling figure of the poet lying outside with huddling geese for company. This was perhaps the least of his eccentricities: he was an unpredictable teacher, allowing lessons to go off in all sorts of unexpected directions, and delighting in the teaching of obscure and sometimes downright peculiar subject matter. But who among us could not have done with a few more teachers like that? These are the teachers who inspired the devotion given to Jean Brodie in Muriel Spark's novel *The Prime of Miss Jean Brodie*, or to John Keating in Tom Schulman's *The Dead Poets' Society*.

It was while teaching at this school that Auden experienced the vision that lay at the heart of "A Summer Night." He later wrote about it in these words:

> One fine summer night in June 1933 I was sitting on a lawn after dinner with three colleagues, two women and one man. We liked each other well enough but we were certainly not intimate friends, nor had any one of us a sexual interest in another. Incidentally, we had not drunk any alcohol. We were talking casually about everyday matters when, quite suddenly and unexpectedly, something happened. I felt myself invaded by a power which, though I consented to it, was irresistible and certainly not mine. For the first time in my life I knew exactly—because, thanks to the power, I was doing it—what it means to love one's neighbour as oneself.

Along with this feeling came a realization of occasions on which he had been spiteful, snobbish, and selfish, but he understood, too, that as long as this state of mind persisted it would be impossible for him to injure another. "The memory of the experience," he wrote, "has not prevented me from making use of others, grossly and often, but it has made it much more difficult for me to deceive myself about what I am up to when I do."

The poem is a vision of agape, that disinterested love of others that has played so important a part in traditional Christian teaching. The Greek word is also sometimes translated as *charity*, its essence being a preparedness to sacrifice one's own interests for the sake of others. Agape urges us to love and value the other not for any reason of personal gain to ourselves but simply because they are our fellow human beings. Nowhere in the poem does Auden use the word itself, but we know that this is his subject, not only from his subsequent explanation of the background to the poem, but also from references at various points in the poem. In the third stanza, after the poet has set the scene and spoken of his good fortune in being where he is ("Where the sexy airs of summer / The bathing hours and the bare arms / The leisured drives through a land of farms / Are good to a newcomer"), he refers to being seated with colleagues in a ring. John Fuller has drawn attention to the significance of this: the early Christian invocation of the spirit of agape involved being seated in a ring—just as Auden and his colleagues are seated here. The evenings, Auden notes, are "enchanted"—precisely because of the effect of agape, we may conclude, and the moon looks down on us all: "Now north and south and east and west/Those I love lie down to rest." Again this feeling of benevolence, of love, is all embracing: all must sleep, and do so with our blessing because of our love for all others. We are human and vulnerable, whatever our individual situation:

The moon looks on them all
The Healers and the brilliant talkers
The eccentrics and the silent walkers
The dumpy and the tall.

Disinterested love of humanity is one thing; erotic love of another is another thing altogether. And yet the two go hand in hand, as Auden pointed out in *Forewords and Afterwords*, where he argued that being in love with one person—in the conventional sense—brings about feelings of goodwill toward others. This will not strike most of us as a novel or dubious proposition: just about everybody who has been in love will surely recall the feeling of benevolence that accompanies that particular emotional state. Who will snap at another just after receiving a love letter, or even an electronic declaration of affection? Who will be churlish to others when basking in the warm glow of having found the perfect partner?

It was while he was teaching at the Downs School that Auden fell in love. This came about at the same time that he was discovering that a sense of political mission was not going to provide him with an adequate structure for his work. Now there was love, and that appeared to fill that gap.

Auden did not hide his homosexuality, even when, as was the case for much of his life, the physical expression of homosexual feeling was illegal. He spoke freely of it to friends whom he judged to be tolerant, and in the poems themselves there are veiled clues as well as fairly specific references to the subject. This particular love affair resulted in one of the most beautiful love poems in the English language, "Lullaby," written in 1937. There is a grave beauty about this

poem—and a tenderness, too, that is movingly
unfeigned:

> Lay your sleeping head, my love,
> Human on my faithless arm;
> Time and fevers burn away
> Individual beauty from
> Thoughtful children, and the grave
> Proves the child ephemeral:
> But in my arms till break of day
> Let the living creature lie,
> Mortal, guilty, but to me
> The entirely beautiful.
>
> Soul and body have no bounds:
> To lovers as they lie upon
> Her tolerant enchanted slope
> In their ordinary swoon,
> Grave the vision Venus sends
> Of supernatural sympathy,
> Universal love and hope;
> While an abstract insight wakes
> Among the glaciers and the rocks
> The hermit's carnal ecstasy.
>
> Certainty, fidelity
> On the stroke of midnight pass

Like vibrations of a bell
And fashionable madmen raise
Their pedantic boring cry:
Every farthing of the cost,
All the dreaded cards foretell,
Shall be paid, but from this night
Not a whisper, not a thought,
Not a kiss nor look be lost.

Beauty, midnight, vision dies:
Let the winds of dawn that blow
Softly round your dreaming head
Such a day of welcome show
Eye and knocking heart may bless,
Find our mortal world enough;
Noons of dryness find you fed
By the involuntary powers,
Night of insult let you pass
Watched by every human love.

This poem stands in stark contrast to the celebration of agape in "A Summer Night." Eros and
his vision are at the heart of this deeply moving
work; this is physical love, accompanied by all
the conflicting emotions to which the flesh can
subject us. This is carnality, but it is carnality of

a most poetic and delicate nature. The poem can be read as one addressed to any lover, and there is nothing in it that reveals the circumstances of its inspiration. It therefore transcends gender—it is neither a gay poem nor a straight poem—and can be appreciated by anybody. The vision of Eros that it speaks of will be instantly recognizable, as what Auden does here is exactly that which he does in so much of his poetry: he puts into words the universal human experience, something that we all will have had but may never have been able to articulate ourselves. Or if we have tried to articulate it, it has never been with quite the same effect; has never seemed so exact, so true.

"Lay your sleeping head," the poem begins, "Human on my faithless arm." The choice of the words *human* and *faithless* shows us exactly what this is, and the words are examples of Auden's ability to use one or two words to portray an entire hinterland of meaning. He wishes his lover, the living creature, to lie in his arms until the break of day, "Mortal, guilty, but to me / The entirely beautiful." Again, a few well-chosen words delineate the moral landscape: beauty counts as far as Eros is concerned, and beauty may override moral scruple. There will be a cost, of course, and it will be exacted, but from this night, he hopes, "not a whisper, not a thought / Not a kiss nor a look be lost." And in the final stanza, the poet expresses his wishes for his lover in terms that are strikingly beautiful:

Let the winds of dawn that blow
Softly round your dreaming head
Such a day of welcome show
Eye and knocking heart may bless . . .

Love is generous, Auden tells us—even sexual love. Eros and agape are two different things, but Venus enables us to feel what he describes as "supernatural sympathy." She also gives us the power to glimpse universal love and hope—not insights that one might always associate with the ordinary human search for sexual gratification but which are there if we open our eyes to them. The mundane physical acts of eating, sleeping, washing one's face, making love can all become something through which we affirm the value of what we find about ourselves in the world. In this respect, reading Auden enables within us feelings of joy and thankfulness, even in the doing of simple things, in much the same way as the appreciation of sublime music or gazing upon a great painting can charge and inspire us somehow to be better than we currently are.

10

That We May Have Dreams and Visions

"A Summer Night" and "Lullaby" are about visions—"Streams," one of a series of nature poems, "Bucolics," written in the early 1950s, contains a memorable account of a dream. The main body of the poem is a celebration of the qualities of water—how it is a playful companion, how it survives man's company (that coarsens roses and dogs, he reminds us), and so on. But almost half the poem relates to a dream the poet has when he falls asleep beside a Yorkshire stream, and this dream itself becomes a vision.

This is how the dream is introduced:

Lately, in that dale of all Yorkshire's the loveliest,
Where, off its fell-side helter-skelter, Kisdon Beck
Jumps into Swale with a boyish shouting,
Sprawled out on grass, I dozed for a second . . .

We might note the poetic effect of inversion in the first line of this excerpt. It is not "in the loveliest of all Yorkshire's dales," but "in that dale of all Yorkshire's the loveliest." The word order here gives greater emphasis to the quality of loveliness and is more powerful for that. The English language allows us some room to play with word order, although not as much as one might imagine. Perhaps there are even more tolerant languages still—languages in which words can be used in any order one wishes, leaving a great deal of ambiguity in the decipherment of most statements. Such languages would not lend themselves to understanding but would make for intriguing ambiguity.

The fact that the stream shouts boyishly is typical of Auden's personalization of the inanimate. We are accustomed to the roaring of rivers, but roaring is something that many inanimate things might do: a jet engine, thunder, a volcano. Shouting is more closely associated with human agency, even if advertisements and notices do it; shouting boyishly is even more clearly a human thing to do. But, dozing by the stream:

And found myself following a croquet tournament

In a calm enclosure, with thrushes popular . . .

More inversion: not "popular with thrushes," a phrase prosaic enough to come from a bird-watching manual, but "with thrushes popular," which is altogether more striking. The lines trigger associations, and memories too. "A croquet tournament" evokes the image of the figures on a lawn, clad in white. White-clad figures in turn stand for something: for calmness, order, purity, and they make me, at least, think of how another game, cricket, used to be played by players dressed entirely in white. Baseball, perhaps, was like that too. Today cricketers appear in outfits of every color, plastered with slogans. The purity has gone, and the cricket field is no longer a place of somnolent, gentle play but one of fast bowling and overt competitiveness. Games in which traditionally nothing much happened, or happened rather slowly—and both cricket and baseball are very similar to one another in that respect—are, I imagine, under pressure to become more dramatic, more of a spectacle.

And then there is the phrase "with thrushes popular." I cannot read this without thinking of a particular picture that I first saw on the cover of a book and then in the Ulster Museum in Belfast. It is Edward Maguire's portrait of the Irish poet Seamus Heaney, painted in 1974, when Heaney was in his mid-thirties. The poet sits behind a small table on which a white cloth has been placed. He is reading a book, which lies open upon the table, and he is looking out directly at the viewer. He is wearing striped trousers of some rough material, and a dark green shirt; he is in a paneled alcove and behind him is a window with astragals. And behind the window, outside, is a luxuriant plant in which, half-hidden by the leaves, three birds are to be seen—thrushes, I think. The significance of the birds is obvious enough, and one does not need *Hall's Dictionary of Subject and Symbol in Art* to interpret it. It is a painting of real presence, but what makes it important for me is that it is a painting *with thrushes popular*. Now, if I sit on the bank of a river that appears teaming with salmon—as I did a year or two ago, when I watched salmon leap exuberantly on their way up a river in northern Scotland—the phrase comes to me and I think, *this is a river with salmon popular*.

He finds himself, then, in that calm enclosure where

of all the players in that cool valley
the best with the mallet was my darling . . .

Onto this scene "in a cream and golden coach drawn by two baby locomotives" comes Eros, a figure described as "the god of mortal doting." A dance is commanded and those present fly round in a ring (the ring again!) until the poet awakes. The final lines of this extraordinary poem are ones of resolution and hope. They show, too, Auden's insight into the consolation provided by a sense of the sacred. The "least of men" are those who lack power and wealth, who are at the bottom of the heap, and yet may find magnificence in a religious myth or a holy place—a sacred river, for instance. I close my eyes and see the Ganges, with crowds of people bathing in its waters, and one of those high Indian skies above, with circling birds, and heat. The dignity of the ordinary person is affirmed by the sacrament of water; a god, a figure of splendor, watches from a shelf in the rock.

. . . But fortunate seemed that
day because of my dream and enlightened
and dearer, water, than ever because of your voice,
    as if

glad—though goodness knows why—to run with
    the human race,
wishing, I thought, the least of men their
figures of splendour, their holy places.

I had read this poem before I experienced the
dream that was for me the equivalent of falling
asleep beside Kisdon Beck. I cannot say that
the poem led to the dream, but what is possible is that the knowledge of the poem made me
receptive—even if at a subconscious level—to a
dream of the sort that I had. I think that is quite
feasible and should not be in the least surprising. The way in which we stock our minds will
surely determine the quality of our experiences,
conscious and subconscious.

In my dream—and it is the most memorable
dream that I have ever had, hence the term *my
dream*—I was somewhere on the west coast of
Scotland. There was a very clear geographical lo-
cus—I was in no doubt as to where I was: on one
of the Hebridean islands that lie off Scotland's
Atlantic coast. They are very beautiful islands—
verdant in summer, purple-tinted by heather in
the autumn—ringed with white sand and water
that is pure and cold and green—the color of
aquamarine. There is a special Gaelic name for

the strip of pasture that joins beach to land here: the *machair*, a lovely word redolent of the gentle landscape in which it occurs. The *machair* has light, sandy soil, has fragments of sea-shell, has carpets of tiny flowers.

I was staying in a house beside the *machair*. In front of this house was a stretch of lawn, and at the edge of the lawn there was a river. By the riverside, its door wide open, was a shed into which I wandered. Inside the shed was a large art nouveau typesetting machine.

I was being called, and I turned away from my discovery of the typesetting machine to make my way back to the house and to our hostess. People in dreams do not always have names, but she did. She was called Mrs. MacGregor.

And then I awoke, and just as Auden did when he awoke from his dream of the croquet match, I felt that I had been vouchsafed a vision. It was a feeling of utter elation and goodwill—in other words, a feeling of agape. I felt bathed in the warm, golden glow of this feeling.

Some year later my wife and I were having dinner with psychiatrist friends in an Edinburgh restaurant. The talk turned to dreams, and I recounted my dream. Unfortunately, as I did so, there was a lull in the conversation at nearby tables, with the result that others heard what I had to say. At the end there was silence. Then one of the psychiatrists said: "I know what your dream is about."

A pin could have been heard to drop.

"Mrs. MacGregor is your mother."

It was exactly the right thing for a psychiatrist to say. The restaurant became noisy again. It was Italian, and the food was delicious. It could not be allowed to get cold. After all, life is not just about visionary dreams, it is about pasta and such matters too. Auden would have agreed with that. The pleasures of the table were important for him; indeed he thought having somebody to cook good meals for one was one of the great goods of this life. Standing at the stove, preparing a sauce, a glass of something at our side, we may well think of Auden and hear his voice extolling the pleasures of domesticity. Yes, he says: take pleasure in exactly this.

11

And Then There Is Nature

Auden's work may be cerebral—his lines are packed with ideas, often densely so—but he is also poet of landscape. His own preferred landscape was the Yorkshire Dales, with its small limestone valleys, and the lead mines lovingly described in "Not in Baedeker," a poem that somehow manages to blend images of Italian religious processions and preening bus drivers with references to English architecture and fauna. But he was sensitive to the charms of very different places too. He did not particularly like mountains, it seems, as he makes clear in his amusing "Mountains," one of his "Bucolics" series. This poem begins,

> I know a retired dentist who only paints mountains
> But the Masters rarely care

That much, who sketch them in beyond a holy
    face . . .

The normal eye, he goes on to say,

    . . . perceives them as a wall
    Between worse and better, like a child scolded in
        France
    Who wishes he were crying on the Italian side of the
        Alps . . .

This image is haunting because it evokes so pow-
erfully what we all must have felt as children—
the conviction that things are better elsewhere
if only we could get there. The powerlessness of
the child is what makes that so poignant: children are trapped in the world created for them
by adults, and for most children the possibility of
escape is remote. The same idea is present in the
Freud poem, where he talks about the child

    . . . unlucky in his little State,
    some hearth where freedom is excluded,
    a hive whose honey is fear and worry . . .

The sympathetic effect of these lines is immediately apparent. Yes, we all knew people like

that when we were ourselves children. I knew a boy at school who lived under the rule of an unduly strict father, and who looked miserable most of the time. His unhappiness must have been compounded by the fact that for several years we shared a mean and sadistic teacher, an Irishman of poisoned temperament who took delight in tormenting his charges. Ireland, the home of many examples of that particular breed of monster, whom she exported in numbers to the rest of the world, has at last set her house in order in that regard and has publicly renounced the Catholic hierarchy that made life so miserable for generations of Irish children. But nobody dared in those days to question such bullies, and the freedom that is more normal these days has come too late for these victims. Auden would have helped, because the whole message of his life and his poetry is the antithesis of cruelty and meanness of spirit.

In the final stanza of "Mountains" the limits of his tolerance for heights is revealed:

> . . . For an uncatlike
> Creature who has gone wrong
> Five minutes on even the nicest mountain
> Are awfully long.

Nor does he like plains, which he says in "Plains" he cannot see without a shudder.

So with what sort of terrain is Auden happiest? Look at where he chose to live. An important part of his life was spent in America, particularly in New York, but the vastness of America certainly did not appeal to him. Italy was more to his taste, and he liked, too, his Austrian village. There was also that short period living in a cottage in the grounds of his old college in Oxford: all small homes with a strong sense of local attachment. It has been suggested that Auden's imagination was not a particularly visual one. While it is true that music and ideas were perhaps more important to him than the visual arts, there is still an extraordinarily rich topography in his works, and landscapes are not only very much present in his poetry but more than mere backdrops to something else. The early landscapes are highly symbolic. "Paysage Moralisé," which was written in 1933, has, after all, a highly revealing title: valleys, mountains, and islands perform an allegorical role—elicit human temptations, moods, disappointments. Later, as this tendency to use landscape symbolically began to play a less prominent role in his poetry, Auden found the human body itself to be a metaphor for place. "The provinces of his body revolted / The squares of his mind were empty" he wrote of the dying Yeats.

The people whom we encounter in Auden's earlier landscapes are often engaged in a quest: they are where they are physically because it is a stage in their journey, the objective of which is the healing of division. They may be lost, as the strangers are in "New Year Letter," standing

> . . . puzzled underneath
> The signpost on the barren heath
> Where the rough mountain track divides
> To silent valleys on all sides . . .

Deserts abound, symbolic of emptiness and aridity; mountains threaten with their violence; paths meander and confuse. As for cities, these can either stand for the alienation and loneliness or, quite the opposite, represent that ideal *civis* to the finding of which the pilgrim's journey is dedicated. In creating a city, or indeed any human habitat, in which it is possible to live in harmony, we reconcile the concerns of spirit and body— which is exactly the goal that Auden sought in his later works. In allowing for the destruction of cities, we create ruins that remind us of the tragic consequences of our divided selves.

Gardens are, of course, something special. It is in the garden that for a brief moment we are allowed to indulge ourselves in music or art: the real world, the world outside, being kept outside by the garden wall. And it is in the walled garden that we might see, of all things, a unicorn

In his *Later Auden*, Edward Mendelson reminds us that Auden's earlier fascination with glaciers and crossroads began in the late 1940s, to be replaced by a much more realistic appreciation of a real world inspired, to begin with, by what he saw in Italy: "his Italian townscapes," Mendelson writes, "had real barbers and buses in them; instead of symbolic winds in allegorical deserts, a real sirocco and long dog days; instead of titanic struggles, a tangible landscape you could settle into."

"In Praise of Limestone," perhaps Auden's best-known poem, represents this point of transition between imaginary landscapes and the real. The poem has been included in numerous anthologies and has been the subject of lengthy critical evaluation. It is a comfortable poem (as befits any paean to limestone), personal, indeed conversational in its tone, and yet it has an extraordinary amount to say about a wide range of subjects: landscape, history, geology, theology, the human body, and sex. It begins in a casually didactic way, with an observation about the properties of limestone—it dissolves in water, Auden reminds us—but becomes increasingly urgent, culminating in echoing, resonant final lines that speak not only to our very human need for love but also to our much more complex spiritual yearnings:

> . . . when I try to imagine a faultless love,
> Or the life to come, what I hear is the murmur
> Of underground streams, what I see is a limestone
>   landscape.

"In Praise of Limestone" is written in the easy, conversational style that became a hallmark of Auden's later work and that goes a long way toward explaining the striking effect that his work has when read aloud. Auden chose to write this poem in regular syllabic meter that eschews the looseness and subjectivity of free verse—verse that does not stick to strict requirements of meter and allows varying lengths of line, different points of stress, and so on. As Edward Mendelson has pointed out, regular syllabic lines became Auden's preferred way of writing about the human body and "the shared meanings signified by the regular metre correspond to the bodily rhythms which everybody has in common and which cannot be imagined as belonging only to the lost past." The reference to the lost past here is to the archaic feel of many poetic meters, which we associate with poems written well before our time. But there is something else in this observation that raises some very interesting issues. The regularity that we see in Auden's verse after "In Praise of Limestone" contributes greatly to the appeal of what he wrote. It is easy on the ear—and ease here has no pejorative implications: the fact that something is easy to listen to does not make it less intellectually significant. Think back to some of the lines already quoted: "The winds must come from somewhere when they blow"—a very regular meter, and one that is widely used in poetry, but very reassuring, like the thrumming of a horse's hooves on the ground, like the oscillation of a clock's pendulum, like the very beating of the pulse. Or perhaps even like the sound of the maternal heartbeat we heard when in the womb; the first sound, no doubt, that any of us heard. Similarly, even when Auden is not using any of the tried and trusted meters of poetry but is writing his regular syllabic lines, there is a rhythm there that seems *essentially right*. Let's go back to the lines at the end of "In Praise of Limestone": "What I hear is the sound of underground streams / What I see is a limestone landscape." Close your eyes and try to imagine the *shape* of these lines. I see a falling, a descent, a softening, with the gentlest of landings at the end. And I feel resolution, calmness, and forgiveness. These feelings are all triggered by the pace of the two lines, but their motion, their tone is one of sharing, the imparting of understanding. A musician might resort to musical concepts to explain this feeling. There is cadence here in exactly the same way as there is cadence in musical composition.

The widespread anthologizing of "In Praise of Limestone" confirms that people like it—but why? Is it just because of the way it sounds, or is it because of its meaning? Answering this question is not easy, largely because the poem's meaning is not immediately apparent; one can read "In Praise of Limestone" and reach the end without being sure what the poem is really about. Is it just about limestone and its comfortable properties? Is it about Italy, or is it in fact about England? Is it about sex? Is it possibly religious?

Some of the most useful insights into this entrancing poem are offered by Edward Mendelson, who goes to some lengths to explain it in the second part of his two-volume study of Auden, *Later Auden*. Mendelson was appointed to the post of Auden's literary executor at an early age. A common mistake that writers make is to appoint a literary executor from the ranks of their coevals. It is understandable why they do that: if anybody can be trusted to be a sympathetic curator of a body of work, surely it will be a friend—and friends tend to be rough contemporaries. But the problem with this is that the literary executor dies either before the writer or not long after. Mendelson was an instructor—an assistant professor—at Yale when he met Auden and impressed the poet with his knowledge of his work. By appointing a young man, Auden ensured the likelihood of a good, long period of attention and curatorship. He also got scholarship and loyalty, both of a particularly high order.

My first meeting with Edward Mendelson had its origin in a letter I received from him a few years after the publication of my Botswana novel, *The No. 1 Ladies' Detective Agency*. I had recently begun a new series of books in which the principal character was an Edinburgh moral philosopher, Isabel Dalhousie, who happened also to be a devotee of the works of W. H. Auden and who was in the habit of thinking about— and quoting—Auden rather a lot. Auden, it seems, had something to say about many of the dilemmas and issues that Isabel encountered in her daily moral life. Mendelson noticed this and wrote me a letter in which he pointed out that in his view W. H. Auden would have agreed with Mma Ramotswe—the heroine of my Botswana novels—on almost every subject.

To hear from Auden's literary executor was something of a thrill—almost as good as hearing from the poet himself, which was, alas, no longer possible. I wrote back and suggested that when I was next in New York—where Mendelson is a professor of English at Columbia University— we might perhaps meet for coffee or lunch. He wrote back and said that he thought this a good idea. A few months later we met in the Russian Tea Room next to the Carnegie Hall. Edward was with his wife, Cheryl, a novelist with whom I shared a New York publisher, and I was with my wife and one of my daughters. In the course of the meeting, I asked Edward whether he would care to appear as a real character in my next Isabel Dalhousie novel. He courteously agreed.

That mention was duly made in the next Dalhousie novel. He and Isabel exchanged letters in that book, with Isabel raising a point about the possible influence of Burns on one of Auden's poems. But then, a year later, in the next Isabel Dalhousie novel, Edward made an even more important appearance, coming to Edinburgh to deliver a lecture on the role of neurotic guilt in Auden's work. In that book, after the lecture he goes to dinner at Isabel's house, where he meets a number of her friends.

I enjoyed creating this link between fiction and reality and indeed have always enjoyed writing real characters into books (with their consent, of course, and always in a positive light). But what followed took this *jeu d'esprit* even further. The following year I invited Edward Mendelson to come to Edinburgh to deliver the lecture he had delivered in the book. Afterward he joined us for dinner with other real people who had appeared as friends of Isabel Dalhousie in the novels. Real life was imitating fiction, but in this case fiction had preceded the real event—a reversal of what might normally be expected to happen.

Later Mendelson came Edinburgh for a longer visit—as the first holder of a fellowship set up in Isabel Dalhousie's name—and we had the opportunity to spend time talking about individual poems. There was so much that I wanted to ask Edward about, and he helpfully explained the meaning of some of the more opaque poems. I was very fortunate, of course, in being able to take advantage in this way of his understanding of poems such as "If I Could Tell You," but even if I had not had this access, I would have been able to find marvelously nuanced explanations in his critical works.

Mendelson sees "In Praise of Limestone" as being not only a series of ruminations on landscape—and it undoubtedly is that—but also a musing on the body, and on the needs of the body. This, he feels, is at the heart of the poem: it is about the flesh, and as the poem progresses it becomes a love poem. The body is always there: it is our home, it is where we are. We may deny that, we may try to rise above the physical yearnings that the flesh inspires, but ultimately we come back to them. Ultimately we are physical creatures. The soft, limestone landscape is mother.

The recognition of these claims of the flesh is what makes Auden seem such an intensely human poet. There are plenty of poets, especially those given to the writing of confessional verse, who are ready to tell us about their particular experience of love. We listen sympathetically and may indeed be touched or inspired by their insights. But few poets transcend the personal when talking about love. They are talking, really, about how *they* felt when they were in love; Auden digs far deeper than that. He talks about love and the flesh as it can be experienced by all of us—he transcends the specific experience in a particular place and time, to get to the heart of what we are. In doing so, though, even if he does not dodge the most complex philosophical and theological issues raised by our human existence, he will still locate everything in the very immediate: in the guts of the living, to use an expression he uses in poem to Yeats. This means that we feel we understand Auden's work even when we do not, or when we need a fair amount of coaching to appreciate fully his references and his meaning.

His concern with the body and its significance can become microscopic. There is a wonderful poem in which Auden turns to the subject of the yeast, bacteria, and viruses that live upon the skin of all of us. "A New Year Greeting" is addressed to these microorganisms, probably the only poem in the English language to concern itself with these invisible presences. The life of these tiny creatures is a perilous one. By what myths, Auden asks, would the priests of these fauna account for

> the hurricanes that come
> twice every twenty-four hours,
> each time I dress or undress,
> when, clinging to keratin rafts,
> whole cities are swept away
> to perish in space, or the Flood
> that scalds to death when I bathe?

This extraordinary poem often sometimes comes back to me when I look, thoughtfully, at human skin—at my own or another's—as I suppose we all do now and then. Their effect is not only to engender a certain curiosity about what the microworld looks like (the poem itself was inspired by Auden's reading of an article in *Scientific American*), but also to make us more aware of what we are. We are individuals with hopes and conceits, but we are also simply flesh, and colonized flesh at that. Again we see Auden's insight into our physicality and the vulnerability that goes with it. And it is humbling, in the real sense of that somewhat abused word.

"A Limestone Landscape" is about the large-scale natural world—the earth on which we live; "A New Year Greeting" is about the microscopic natural world. What about the world in-between—the natural world of animals? There are plenty of animals in Auden's poems—rather unexpectedly, perhaps. Auden's world encompasses music, psychology, and theology, but one would not have thought that there would be many animals. And yet they are there, either as bit players or, in the later poems, as the principal subject of the poem. There are plenty of dogs, perhaps most famously in his well-known poem about the banality of suffering, "Musée des Beaux Arts," where "the dogs go on with their doggy life" while the small, unobserved tragedy of Icarus falling into the water occurs in the background. Surprisingly, for a poet who personalizes all sorts of inanimate objects (talking streams, rocks, and so on), few of the animal references are anthropomorphic. Dogs seem to represent anarchy and threat, or sometimes just sheer exuberance. Auden's iconography of dogs differs little from the use of dogs in painting, where their iconographic role includes domesticity and loyalty. I have in my study a Dutch painting of a young boy and his dog. There are quite a few iconographic references in the picture—an hourglass and a spear being the obvious ones—but there is also a dog, and there is no doubt about its significance. The dog stands up on its hind legs, its forelegs resting against the boy's skirts (the boy is about six, and at that time, the seventeenth century, small boys were dressed in skirts); the boy's future is alluded to by the hourglass, his costly garb, and the spear; the dog the represents the companionship and loyalty that will see him through this future.

Auden's dogs may be violent and rumbustious, but they are also fun and friendly. In Caliban's address to the audience in *The Sea and the Mirror* he refers to a "green kingdom, where the steam rollers are as friendly as the farm dogs." And in "A Bad Night (a lexical exercise)" we see Auden in playful form coming up with a new adjective for the dogs owned by the "infrequent shepherds, sloomy of face." These are "scaddle dogs," a term that will send all of us to the dictionary to discover that *scaddle*, when applied to an animal, means badly behaved or skittish. *Sloomy*, which is one of those words we feel we know the meaning of even if we do not—describes the look of one who is sleepy or sluggish. Although not a word in everyday use, it crops up in John Clare, who says

"O'er pathless plains, at early hours, The sleepy rustic sloomy goes." The picture is clear enough: sloomy seems right for the image of somebody going to work at an unearthly hour but does not quite fit the modern pastoralist who will have to be energetic if he is to survive the mechanized agriculture of our age. In that same poem, Auden thinks he will defeat us with the line "far he must hirple." That may bring out the dictionary for many, but not in Scotland, where *hirple* is a Scots word that is in everyday use. It means to limp, and it is what one does when one has pulled a tendon. A *scaddle* dog would certainly *hirple* if his skittishness caused him to overexert himself and hurt a paw.

There are countless other instances of Auden's delight in using words on the cusp of that damning dictionary verdict *archaic*. Never does one get the impression that these words are being used in a showy way: they are there deliberately, and sometimes, no doubt, they are chosen not only for their pleasurable quality but because they have the right number of syllables for the line, but they are never used to impress. Rather, they are used to express and share the poet's delight in the sheer richness of the English language. In my own reading of Auden I was led to *widdershins* (counterclockwise) and *deasil* (clockwise)—in "Lakes" he says that "sly foreign ministers" should always meet beside a lake because

> . . . whether they walk widdershins or deasil,
> the path will yoke their shoulders to one liquid
>   centre,
> Like two old donkeys pumping as they plod;
> such physical compassion may not guarantee
> a marriage for their armies, but it helps . . .

Then there is the water in "Streams" that makes fun of our human feuds

> by opposing identical banks
> and transferring the loam from Huppim
> to Muppim and back each time you crankle.

Crankle is not the difficulty here—onomatopoeic words, or words that are close to onomatopoeic, usually make their meaning clear enough, but Huppim and Muppim? A biblical reference: the sons of Benjamin, it seems, rather than, as in our ignorance we might suspect, children's puppets.

Dogs occur, as do other animals, with some frequency in Auden's late poems. The appearance of animals at this stage emphasizes the concern he had long harbored, but which is now very much to the fore, with the celebration of the comfortable certainties of domestic life. Animals are part of that life, but they are more than mere furniture; they have their own lives to lead, and, unlike us, these lives are led in harmony with the world: they are "naturally good"—to use the phrase that Auden chose to describe healthy plants and animals. This idea of the natural goodness is also strikingly present in a scene from one of Iris Murdoch's novels, *The Philosopher's Pupil*, in which the characters attend a Quaker meeting and are all moved and morally affected by the insights of what is said by there—all except the small papillon dog, Zed, smuggled in by the boy who owns him: the dog, "being composed of pure goodness," is unchanged.

Auden wrote "Talking to Dogs" in 1970. It is a musing on canine qualities that will strike an immediate chord with the dog owner who has turned, as all such must on occasion do, to the dog for support or encouragement. And dogs never let us down in that respect: they understand, even when they so patently are incapable of making sense of what we tell them. That is not the point, of course; telling a friend of one's troubles does not require any critical evaluation by the friend—in such circumstances we are really talking to ourselves. Auden expresses this nicely:

Being quicker to sense unhappiness
Without having to be told the dreary
Details or who is to blame, in dark hours
Your silence may be of more help than many
Two-legged comforters . . .

A year later he wrote "Talking to Mice," a poem that echoes that other great poem about mice, Robert Burns's "Ode to a Mouse," written in 1785. Burns reflects on a mouse that he, the plowman, has disturbed in his plowing of a field and makes the widely quoted observation that "the best-laid schemes of mice and men / gang aft agley (often go wrong)"—as they undoubtedly do, from the failure of a trivial social arrangement—a plan to meet for lunch, defeated by heavy traffic—to the spectacular disaster of a dysfunctional rocket launch. But it is other lines from this poem that lodge in my mind, lines of apology for what we do to the creatures around us: "I'm truly sorry man's dominion / Has broken nature's social union." These lines often come back to me, reproachfully, each time I do something that abruptly brings to an end the life of some tiny creature: a snail inadvertently crushed to death underfoot, a spider deliberately washed down the drain by what must seem to it a tsunami of bathwater. We have to be indifferent to the death of insects and other creatures if we are to eat food from commercially produced crops, which rely on insecticides, let alone if we scale the food chain to eat bacon or fish. But we tuck away such knowledge and forget the horrors of the slaughterhouse, its blood and viscera and squealing, when we tackle with relish our chicken sandwich or our hamburger.

Auden's "Talking to Mice" is not dissimilar to Burns's poem in its concern with the relationship between man and mouse. Burns destroyed the mouse's world when his plow cut through its tiny home; Auden, while able to live in good-neighborliness with two household mice, cannot permit a vastly enlarged family of mice to remain at liberty and resorts to a mousetrap to dispose of them, which it does, with success, fatally fooling the mice "who would never believe an unusual object pertaining to men could be there for a sinister purpose." He had no talent for murder, he goes on to say, but why, then, should the mice be killed? The answer is one that harkens back to the way the State behaves: the mice have been killed

... For *raisons d'État*. As
   householders we had behaved exactly as every State
      does
   when there is something It wants, and a minor one
      gets in the way.

Yes, of course that happens, and we can all find instances of it in our local lives. The modern world may be a slightly safer place for "minor ones"—the development of human rights over the past half-century has done a great deal to further that—but the inclinations of the State to which Auden refers are still there.

In this poem, as in so much of his work, the small leads to the bigger; in the quotidian detail we can see the shape of something much larger: a greater truth, a more profound insight.

12

Auden as a Guide to the Living of One's Life

He Helps Us to Have Spiritual Purpose, and to Love

In "As I Walked Out One Evening" Auden gives us two memorable lines about the transience of our lives: "In headaches and in worry / Vaguely life leaks away." For most of us that is probably true—at least for part of the time. Our life is short and seems all the shorter the closer one comes to its end. We would like to do great things; we would like to lead a life that is full of meaning and purpose, but there are few of us who achieve that—rather, we struggle to catch up with lives the course of which is determined by chance, by the vagaries of fate. As a result, we may live our days suspecting that we are not getting from life all that we might. The famous question *Is this all there is?* sums up that dissatisfied, possibly puzzled feeling rather succinctly.

Of course there are several ways of filling this empty core at the heart of our existence. One of these is religious belief, and Auden was one who chose this as his preferred solution to emptiness. He embraced Christian belief—or re-embraced it—when it dawned on him that liberal humanism had failed to prevent the moral disaster of fascism and the horrors it brought. He was nudged in that direction in a famous incident in which he witnessed, at a cinema in New York, the German audience cheering on the killing of Poles. In "New Year Letter" he considered the notion of the Kierkegaardian leap into faith: the act of commitment that enables us to assert a position that reason alone might not be able to justify. Thereafter he knew what belief he would profess, even if the rational dissection of the tenets of that belief might produce doubt or incredulity. Many people take that view, electing to believe in something that may wither under close scrutiny but that nonetheless represents an engaged response to evil and emptiness. And why should they not do this? The rationalist will argue that we should face up to the reality of our position, even if that reality offers us no comfort. A fond belief in something that we cannot prove, the rationalist would argue, amounts to nothing more than self-delusion; far better to be adult, to face up to the facts of our existence and use humanistic values to justify and inform the struggle for a better world.

It is certainly possible to see the logic of such a position. Courage in facing up to the fact that we have no life other than this one, that there is no divine intervention in human affairs, and that we can expect no help might well be expected to shock us into moral improvement. And yet, in practice, such a view has not done that. When Auden decided that science and psychology, along with the liberal humanistic values they proclaimed, were powerless in the face of real evil, he chose to commit himself to a system of belief that gave grounds for the pursuit of the good, and to a set of rituals that embodied that notion of the good; by identifying, then, with a power for good, we give our own weak spirit a strengthening boost. That may amount to whistling in the dark, but if its effect is to give a sense of moral purpose and thus enable us to lead lives that have moral shape, then one might be justified in asking what is wrong with that.

I can understand the discomfort of the rationalist over this. I can see, too, the argument that ultimately it is better to be truthful to ourselves and others about everything, but I wonder whether the destruction of Western spirituality has ultimately enriched us more than it has impoverished us. I believe that the materialism that has become the prevailing value of many post-Christian Western societies has not brought us any greater happiness—indeed its reductionist effect appears to have brought widespread alienation. The material appetites can never be satisfied; we shall never be made happier or more fulfilled simply by possessing the latest electronic gadgets or being able to afford bigger and better material things. That simply will not happen; in fact, the outcome of a materialist philosophy will be quite the opposite. Auden would agree with that, and if today we seek to understand his spiritual quest, as well as the other quests that played an important part of his life, we might be encouraged to embark on similar quests ourselves. The results may be distinctive for each of us; not everybody is going to end up, as Auden did, in the Anglican Church or indeed in any church. The spiritual life can be cultivated in all sorts of ways: through music, through poetry, through the cherishing of others or, more broadly, the appreciation and understanding of nature. It helps, though, to have the support of others in our striving, and so it may be more effective to participate in the institutional effort that organized religion involves—but this is not necessary. Nor, I think, is it necessary to believe in a personal god of the sort that we find in Christian doctrine. Religions are full of myths and things that defy belief; these things can clutter and obscure, can put off those who might otherwise find solace or purpose in religious practice. We do not have to believe them, though; we can see them for what they are—expressions of value—and live with them because they have been thought necessary in the past, as signposts to something that would otherwise be too difficult to explain, or because some find them helpful in the cultivating of a spiritual life. We can act, then, as if they were true, although we know they are not, embracing the purpose and dignity they give to our lives, the example they set. That is not dishonest, nor is it cowardly; it is easier to proclaim meaninglessness than it is to assert meaning or to see the meaning in symbolic myths; it is easier to be cynical and dismissive than it is to assert the primacy of the good. We should not see Auden's adoption of a Christian position as a retreat into the comfort of a sheltering creed—it was a highly intellectualized process; it was for him the only solution, the only thing that could impose on life the sense of order and meaning he sought. This was the reaction of a critical, acute mind, not a clutching at a straw of comfort.

There is very short poem by Auden in which I take great comfort. "The More Loving One," written in 1957, can be read at one level as a poignant, but not particularly complicated, reflection on unrequited love. It is considerably more than that, though: it is an acceptance that in the face of meaninglessness or indifference it is still possible to be engaged in the world—it is still possible to love. These are the first two stanzas of this curious little poem:

> Looking up at the stars, I know quite well
> That, for all they care, I can go to hell,
> But on earth indifference is the least
> We have to dread from man or beast.

How should we like it were stars to burn

With a passion for us we could not return?

If equal affection cannot be,

Let the more loving one be me.

At first blush there seems to be nothing complicated about these lines. The argument can be summed up as follows: the stars have no interest in us—there are some things for which our human concerns are a matter of complete indifference; our life is nothing to them. In our earthly lives, though, indifference is not too bad—there are plenty of things that can do us a great deal more harm than can indifference. But what if we are faced with the opposite of indifference—a strong passion that we cannot reciprocate? It is better then, Auden suggests, to be the giver of love rather than its object.

But can he really mean that? Can it really be true that the person who burns with passion for one who does not return it is better placed than the nonreciprocating object of his or her love? I would have thought that the misery of such a situation is very clear. The person who loves another who cannot or will not love him or her back is surely to be pitied, and most of us would probably not wish to be that person. So

·

what Auden suggests here flies in the face of our common experience of the pain of unrequited love, unless he is suggesting that it is particularly uncomfortable to be the subject of love that one does not want. He probably does mean that, because Auden was himself the more loving one in his long relationship with Chester Kallman, and perhaps that is what he accepted, and indeed wanted. Why? Because to love another who is unworthy of one's love or who will not respond to it is a mature act of moral commitment of precisely the sort that Auden valued and that he himself practiced in his relationship with Kallman. Kallman was unfaithful to him, and indeed there was a moment when Auden may have came close to killing him—a shocking revelation that he was later to allude to in a verse letter to Kallman. We cannot be completely certain of the facts, but according to one account Auden had his hands poised above the throat of his sleeping lover and could easily have proceeded to throttle him but did not.

There is another way in which we can read the lines "If equal affection cannot be, / Let the more loving one be me." This reading has nothing to do with psychological comfort but is concerned with, rather, the need that we have to love others in spite of what they feel about us. It would be best if we could all love one another to the same degree, but that will not be possible. Some, therefore, will not love us, but that does not mean that we should fail to love them. To say *let the more loving one be me* is to express the hope that we shall rise above the indifference of others, and perhaps even above their animosity, and love them more than they love us. Surely that is true—and surely even if this reading takes those words out of context, the message is a profoundly moving and inspiring one.

He Reminds Us of Community, and of How Our Life May Be Given Meaning through Everyday Things

This is one of the greatest gifts that Auden has for us. Auden has been described as a Horatian poet—a poet in the tradition of Horace, the Roman port of the Augustan age whose work, particularly his *Odes*, expresses his love and gratitude for the life of the untroubled farmer, happy with his lot in life, savoring the pleasures of the tables, enjoying the company and conversation of friends, and bringing his poetic sensibility to bear on the everyday matters of our domestic life. Alan Jacobs has traced Auden's journey to this Horatian position in his eminently readable account of the poet's career, *What Became of Wystan?* In particular, Jacobs points out the striking similarities between Horace's eulogizing of his Sabine farm in the *Satires* and Auden's lines in "Thansgiving for a Habitat." Horace says:

> This is what I had prayed for: a small piece of land
> With a garden, a fresh flowing spring of water at
>   hand
> Near the house . . .
> It's perfect. I ask for nothing else, except to implore,
> O Son of Maia, that you make these blessings my
>   own
> For the rest of my life . . .

And almost two thousand years later, Auden says of his cottage in Austria,

> . . . I, a transplant
> from overseas, at last am dominant
> Over three acres and a blooming
> conurbation of country lives . . .
>
> . . . .

> What I dared not hope or fight for
> is in my fifties, mine, a toft-and-croft
> where I needn't, ever, be at home to
> those I am not at home with . . .

A poet in the Horatian tradition need not necessarily be insensitive to the major issues of the day but is nonetheless likely to be concerned with the personal moral life—with the effort that we all must make to live with our private conscience. This will result in a focus on our own lives as people engaging with others, making choices, responding to art, being a citizen, and so on. This focus may lead to gratitude of the sort that Horace voiced—and that Auden expresses too. Auden reminds us to be grateful, and that is something that we increasingly need to be reminded of in a culture of expectation and entitlement. Consumerist culture has encouraged us to complain—we have become very good at that—but it does not encourage us to say thank you. As a result, expressions of gratitude may even strike us today as surprising—something worthy of remark. But why not say thank you? Perhaps we do not express gratitude because we do not think that we have anything to be grateful for. In which case, Auden certainly helps, because his poems after 1940 tend to be poems of celebration, written with great charity and with love for the ordinary pleasures of life. That message is immensely powerful, and even if it is Horatian in tone, it is more potent in its moral effect that any quantity of impassioned more political verse spelling out the features of injustice and suffering. The fact that one concentrates on the cultivation and appreciation of the personal life does not mean that one will be any the less dismayed than those who adopt a more publicly engaged position; you have to cherish something before you can truly defend it.

His particular insight was that we need to be *at home*; all his concerns with division within ourselves, with the tragic flaws in our nature, with the thwarting of love—all these point to the need that he felt we had within us to locate ourselves in a place we could live in with love, with people with whom we could share. This insight was evident in the early Auden but became stronger and more clearly expressed with the passage of time. It is there, explicitly stated, in that line in "Streams" in which he talks about the need that people have for their holy places; it suffuses the later poems in which he celebrates domesticity, the living space, our habitat. His nightmare was an absence of the sense of belonging—the life of the anonymous city in which we are all strangers, largely indifferent to one another. Auden lived in a large city, New York, but combated the loneliness of such a life by creating community through friendships and intellectual exchange. That is what we, too, must do; indeed that is what we shall be increasingly obliged to do in a world in which globalization sweeps away the power of the local to protect our sense of who we are and where we come from.

Preserving the human scale of our lives in the face of the onslaught of globalization and its bland culture cannot be achieved by legislative fiat. The declared cultural policy of states may be to protect or enhance local culture—France does that, as does Canada, to an extent—but such measures sometimes seem to be no more than the putting of a finger in a dike of a near-universal popular culture. It is very difficult to protect ourselves from fast-food chains or standardized coffee bars; it is equally difficult to keep fragile or threatened cultures alive in the face of blandishments of powerful offerings from far away. Many people today lead cultural lives that are rendered shallow because the things that have been authentic to their particular place are overshadowed by things made or done for them elsewhere, a long way from where they are, and having no ties to their past. That may be largely inevitable, given technological change, but it involves the loss of possibilities of feeling and belonging and fosters a consequent impoverishment of spirit. We can restore the power of the local by resisting the claims of those forces that would take away from us our control of our local lives. It is not particularly easy, but victories can be achieved against impersonal agencies, against empires even, by people asserting the value of what is local to them and taking back the power to control it. The Soviet Union's grip on Eastern Europe was ultimately weakened by just that, and the process of resisting distant power will repeat itself elsewhere unless people become too dehumanized to resist. But what they have to have to inspire them in such efforts is a culture that is real and valuable to *them*. By helping us to understand our choices, by illuminating our life and encouraging us to feel grateful for it, Auden assists the cause of freedom.

On his memorial in Westminster Abbey are inscribed the words *In the prison of his days / Teach the free man how to praise.* I remember when I first read that these lines had been chosen for that memorial, I was not sure I understood why. Now I understand.

I have learned so much from this poet. I have been transported by his words. My life has been enriched by his language. I have stopped and thought, and thought, over so many of his lines. He can be with us in every part of our lives, showing us how rich life can be, and how precious. For that, I am more grateful to him than I can ever say.